VELÁZQUEZ

VELÁZQUEZ

Enrique Lafuente Ferrari

SKIRA
RIZZOLI
NEW YORK

First published 1960
First paperback edition 1988

Published in the United States of America in 1988 by

Rizzoli INTERNATIONAL PUBLICATIONS, INC.
597 Fifth Avenue/New York 10017

© 1988 by Editions d'Art Albert Skira S.A., Geneva

Printed in Switzerland

Library of Congress Cataloging-in-Publication Data

Lafuente Ferrari, Enrique
     Velázquez / Enrique Lafuente Ferrari
          p.   cm.
     Translated from the French version of the original Spanish.
     Bibliography: p.
     ISBN 0-8478-0948-X (pbk.): $25.00
          1. Velázquez, Diego. 1599-1660.   2. Painters—Spain—Biography.
3. Painting, Spanish.   4. Painting, Modern—17th-18th centuries
Spain.   I. Title.
ND813.V4L3   1988
759.6—dc19   87-37699
                                                   CIP

CONTENTS

Self-Portrait, c. 1631. Uffizi, Florence.

A SILHOUETTE OF THE MAN

"The life of Velázquez is one of the simplest a man ever lived... and... one of the most enigmatic, most difficult to understand that one can meet with."

JOSÉ ORTEGA Y GASSET.

Less than a year after the death of King Philip II, Diego Velázquez was born in Seville, under the silky sky of an Andalusian summer. He was baptized on June 6, 1599. His father, Juan Rodríguez de Silva, came of a family of Portuguese hidalgos, native to Porto, who had settled in Seville, at that time the richest city in Spain. His mother, Jerónima Velázquez, whose name he took and made famous, was a native of Seville; she too, apparently, was of noble birth.

Seville was a flourishing art center. The many local schools of the fifteenth century had gradually come to be concentrated in a few leading cities: Toledo, the old Spanish capital, already sinking into irremediable decay; Seville, market town of a rich agricultural region and hub of overseas trade with the Americas; Valencia, the main Spanish seaport on the Mediterranean; and Madrid, seat of the monarchy under Philip II and capital of the country after 1606.

In 1610, at the age of eleven, Velázquez began his apprenticeship in the studio of the painter Francisco Pacheco, a mediocre artist but one who enjoyed great prestige in Seville; to him we owe the most interesting information we have about his young disciple. A competent, unpretentious painter, a cultivated man of letters and an art theorist, Pacheco published in Seville in 1649 a book entitled *Arte de la pintura*, a belated echo of mannerist doctrines. He had read all the treatises of the Renaissance, and in his book quotations from these alternate with chapters on technique which have much to tell us about the methods and working habits of the painters of his day. Nephew of a humanist prelate, Pacheco gathered around him a circle of cultivated friends and held open house to some of the best-known poets and writers of Spain. He was an influential man and his pupil early enjoyed the benefit of his friendships. An incidental remark dropped by Pacheco substantiates the tradition that Velázquez first studied under Francisco Herrera the Elder, a bolder, more modern-minded painter than the cautious Pacheco.

When the six-year bond of apprenticeship came to an end in 1617, Velázquez passed his examination before Pacheco and the painter Juan de Uceda and qualified as a full-fledged master. A year later he married Pacheco's daughter Juana. Pacheco must have been a better teacher than painter; he was broad-minded enough not to impose an outmoded credo on his pupil. Velázquez, for his part, had early given every sign of his bent toward a kind of painting very different from the provincial academicism of his environment. Now, a married man before his nineteenth birthday, the young artist began his professional career in the modest circumstances in which the painters of Seville lived and worked: with hopes, that is, of obtaining orders for altar pictures from the monasteries, and occasionally for portraits. But everything goes to show that he was not made for this routine. And fortune, as it so happened, was soon to favor him. Already a qualified master, though very young, he employed apprentices in his studio. Two daughters were born to him: Francisca and Ignacia. A few months after the birth of the latter occurred the event that was to change the painter's life: the accession of Philip IV to the Spanish throne.

Philip III had been a colorless, devoutly religious king, weak-willed and dull-witted; affairs of state he left in the hands of a strong man, the Duke of Lerma, thus breaking the tradition of hard work and personal government handed down by the bureaucratic king Philip II. The country had disapproved of this relinquishment of power and wished for a change. But things were not destined to change for the better. For Seville, nevertheless, the new reign began auspiciously. Philip IV, the second do-nothing king of the House of Austria, cared no more than his father for the exercise of power, and he soon left the administration in the hands of a great Sevillian nobleman, Don Gaspar de Guzmán, Count-Duke of Olivares. As governor of the Alcázar of Seville, Don

Gaspar paid court to the Duke of Lerma and became gentleman in waiting to the heir apparent, the future Philip IV, whose favor he soon won. This was an unmerited piece of good fortune for him, and a disaster for Spain. He was an unctuous flatterer, a bungling, incompetent administrator, but possessed with the passion for authority so common among Spanish politicians, whose main object seems to be the preservation of their own power rather than the good of the country. At the death of his uncle Don Gaspar de Zuñiga, Olivares inherited the royal seal; soon he was prime minister, and all-powerful. He lived to witness and contribute to the final decay of the Habsburgs in Spain.

Around the Andalusian nobleman, now raised to power, gathered at once a whole clique of Sevillians, most of them friends of Francisco Pacheco: the poet Rioja who had acted as a witness at Velázquez' wedding; Don Luis de Fonseca, an ecclesiastic, gentleman of the king's bedchamber, and an amateur of painting; and the Alcázar brothers. Pacheco saw an opportunity here of introducing his son-in-law at court; he had faith in his talent and his ability as a portraitist. In 1622 Velázquez paid his first visit to Madrid and gained admittance to the circle of Olivares' friends. He only succeeded in seeing the Escorial and its collections and in painting a portrait of Luis de Góngora, the great Baroque poet. The inner circles of the court were still closed to him. But a year later his luck turned. Olivares himself summoned him to Madrid. His best introduction there proved to be the portrait he made of Fonseca; the picture created a sensation in the palace. Olivares contrived to bring it to the king's attention and Philip was dazzled by the mastery of the young man from Seville. He condescended to have his own portrait painted by him; it was finished on August 30, 1623, and was a complete success. Velázquez was taken into the king's service, to the exclusion of all other painters, and was ordered to make his home at court.

It was not only his art, but his personal appearance, his noble birth, his simplicity, the urbanity of his manners that won over the king. For the next thirty-seven years, untiringly, Velázquez painted his royal model. Philip was the jaded scion of a dynasty blighted by interbreeding: pale and blond, as averse to the business of governing as he was fond of hunting, theatricals, and good-looking women. It took him twenty years to wake up to the incapacity of his prime minister and the ruinous decay of his power; when at last he tried to mend matters it was late in the day. If Philip IV has a title to the gratitude of posterity, he owes it to his generous patronage of Velázquez, and even more to his friendship for him. And, unusual for the Spanish court, nothing ever belied or clouded the favor Velázquez enjoyed. The king was true to his painter and never parted with him, not only employing him as a portraitist but opening to him the career of a palace official. Very high was the honor paid him, even though it encroached a little on his work as an artist. The very year of his arrival at court, Velázquez had as a sitter the Prince of Wales, the future Charles I of England, then on a visit to Madrid, seeking to obtain the hand of an infanta and thus to cement an alliance. Here was the heir of Queen Elizabeth soliciting the friendship of Spain! The new reign was beginning under the fairest auspices, which events, however, failed to justify.

The prompt success of the young Velázquez won him both friends and enemies. Among the most hostile to him was Vicente Carducho, an artist of Italian extraction who had been able to cut the figure of a leader at court until Velázquez arrived. He was a belated mannerist and a timid realist, more cultured than talented; he wrote some *Diálogos sobra la pintura*, published in 1633, which reveal, when read between the lines, how jealous the old academic painter was of the young revolutionary. In the early years of his official career in Madrid, Velázquez had his first —and last—taste of popular success. He had made an equestrian portrait of the king, against a landscape background, which was so much admired by all who saw it that Philip consented to have the painting exhibited in public at the gate of a monastery beside the Puerta del Sol, a singular precedent of the open-air exhibitions of today. The result was the triumph of a new manner of painting. The court poets vied with each other in singing the praises of this portrait, which has not come down to us.

This popular triumph was soon followed by the official rebuff of Velázquez' rivals in a competition organized at the palace. The new Spanish painting was now to prevail over the academicism of the Italians hitherto sponsored by the court. A historical theme was set for the competing artists to treat: the *Expulsion of the Moriscoes*, a stern political measure taken by Philip III in 1609. Velázquez had to compete with Carducho, Caxes and Nardi. The jury was composed of Italians, but they unhesitatingly awarded him first prize. This was in 1627. Further rewards were in store for him: in addition to small favors, the king established him on an intimate footing at court and appointed him Gentleman Usher. The provincial painter of humble still lifes, the precocious portraitist turned painter of historical pictures, now held the office that made him the king's closest confidant. Apartments were set aside for him in the palace and the king took to visiting his studio, watched him paint and chatted with him.

Rubens, court painter to the Infanta Isabella, governor of the Low Countries, came to Madrid in 1628 on an unofficial diplomatic mission. Pacheco asserts that the Flemish master was already in correspondence with Velázquez. He now became his friend, and with him visited the Escorial and the royal collections. In their long talks together Rubens dwelt nostalgically on years spent in Italy in his youth, and filled Velázquez with a desire to see the marvels of Italy for himself and perfect his natural gifts by studying the Old Masters. As soon as he had put the finishing touches on his *Triumph of Bacchus*, Velázquez obtained from the king leave to travel and a grant to defray his expenses. Olivares gave him letters of recommendation to various Italian courts.

He travelled in an official capacity, accompanying Ambrosio Spinola, the great Genoese general in the service of Spain, who died soon afterwards at the siege of Casale. Velázquez was eager to reach Venice, being attracted above all by the works of Tintoretto, several of which he copied. From Venice, by way of Ferrara, Loreto and Bologna, he went to Rome. The itinerary he followed is marked out for us by the dispatches of the Spanish ambassadors who attended him at each stage of his journey, for he was an important person at the court. In Rome he was given an apartment in the Vatican and he stayed for a time at the Villa Medici, where he brooded in the gardens among cypresses and roses. At Naples he met Ribera. Velázquez was the first Spanish artist to meet some of his greatest colleagues. He steeped himself in impressions of art and painting. These were to remain indelibly graven on the memory of the shy and silent Velázquez. Italy, which left such nostalgic associations in the mind of Cervantes, impressed itself even more deeply on this master of the visual world.

By the beginning of January 1631 he was back in Madrid. Olivares, now undisputed dictator, was playing at power politics and encouraging the amusements of the weak-willed king. The court's favorite pleasure haunt was the palace of Buen Retiro. Receptions, theatricals, water pageants and nocturnal entertainments followed one another in an atmosphere of obsequious flattery. Costly renovations were under way and the palace was soon filled with the works of art which his courtiers had been invited to present to the king. The great Salón de los Reinos was to be decorated with military scenes, representing Spanish feats of arms in the reign of Philip IV from the Palatinate to the Americas. The duke, ostensibly flattering the king, was really preparing to glorify his own government. All the painters of any repute were set to work. Even the diffident Zurbarán, whom Velázquez had known from his prentice years, was summoned from Seville. Velázquez himself was painting portrait after portrait, besides a historical picture: *The Surrender of Breda*, or *The Lances*. In 1635 a chorus of court poets hymned the beauties of the country palace, the triumphs of the king, and the glorious achievements of the minister. The climax of this ill-founded optimism came with the victory won by the Infante Don Fernando, the king's brother, at the battle of Nördlingen (1634).

Nothing could abate Philip's delight in merry-making, hunting, poetry contests, and works of art. With the Buen Retiro well enough appointed to suit his taste, he conceived the idea of decorating the Torre de la Parada, a hunting lodge in the Pardo woods. This time it was not

Cardinal Borgia, c. 1643. Black chalk.
Academia de San Fernando, Madrid.

for Spanish artists to do the work; what the king now fancied was an array of female nudes to embellish this small private retreat. The main commission went to Rubens, and with the Metamorphoses of Ovid as his theme, he set his studio to work. Several rooms in the Prado are today filled with the remains of these decorations. Velázquez seconded the king in seeing this vast artistic program carried out, to the detriment at times of his own work.

But things were drawing to a crisis in Spain. By the early 1640s, consistently misgoverned ever since the king had withdrawn to Buen Retiro, the Spanish empire was shaken to its foundations. Catalonia and Portugal were in open rebellion, conspiracies in Andalusia and Aragon miscarried. French armies were advancing on the Ebro. Meanwhile, Olivares was preoccupied with perpetuating his fame in an equestrian portrait ordered from Velázquez to commemorate a victory won in 1639 at the defense of Fuenterrabia. The king continued to indulge in his pleasures at Buen Retiro, and one day, like a presage of evil, fire broke out in the palace. The people grew restless, and discontent spread. The economic situation was ruinous. Not even the king's household could make ends meet. Salaries were overdue. We find Velázquez claiming arrears for paintings finished and delivered. As early as 1630 an Italian ambassador at Madrid could write: "The King pays no one."

Velázquez married off his daughter in 1634, and from then on, in the person of his son-in-law Juan del Mazo, he had an able assistant to relieve him of routine work and the replicas so often requested of him. His official duties at the palace occupied the bulk of his time. Yet he painted steadily, mostly portraits, countless portraits, for presentation to foreign courts.

The hour of decision had come. Condé's victory at Rocroi (1643) dealt a fatal blow to Spanish arms and Olivares' position became untenable. The war in Catalonia obliged the king to bestir himself to the extent of inspecting his troops in the field in 1642. Velázquez accompanied him to Saragossa. But the situation got no better, and by 1643 Philip had no alternative but to dismiss Olivares.

Velázquez' position was unaffected by the disgrace of the man who had first patronized him. The king esteemed him as a friend and fresh responsibilities devolved upon him. Again he accompanied his master into Aragon and Catalonia, and at Fraga in 1644 he painted one of his finest portraits of him. They were travelling again in 1645 and 1646. Appointed Gentleman of the Bedchamber, his new duties required his constant attendance on the king. In 1645 Lérida was recaptured, but in the following year Sicily revolted; and what was worse, Prince Don Baltasar Carlos died, the king's eldest son and heir to the throne, the last hope of the dynasty, an intelligent boy of great promise, of whom Velázquez had made such charming portraits. Revolt broke out in Naples. The world seemed to be collapsing around the king. The Peace of Westphalia in 1648 was the first open admission of the decay of Spanish power.

Philip IV consoled himself with comedies and painting. Had he not been a king, he would have been a poet, a collector, a lover of life; he had the makings of an artist; as a king he was a failure and the undoing

View of Granada, 1648. Pen and sepia. Biblioteca Nacional, Madrid.

of his country. As he made plans to form a picture gallery, Velázquez volunteered to go to Italy and buy the masterpieces of painting and statuary which would give new luster to the royal collections. Letters were dispatched in the king's name to the Spanish ambassadors at Italian courts recommending Velázquez to their care and protection. He sailed from Málaga on January 21, 1649, joining on board ship the official mission headed by the Duke of Najera, bound for Trent to fetch the new Austrian wife of the king, who was anxious to provide an heir to his throne. Landing at Genoa on February 11, Velázquez parted company with the embassy and proceeded to revisit the Italian cities that had captivated him twenty years before: Milan, Padua, Venice, Modena, Rome, Naples.

Received in Venice as the king's envoy and a notability, known to have come in search of major works of art, he was attended on and paid homage to. He was even "interviewed"—a Baroque interview, befitting the times, and in verse, written in the Venetian dialect and included by Marco Boschini in his book *La Carta del navegar pitoresco*, published in Venice years later in 1660. Here is the description it gives of Velázquez:

Cavalier, che spirava un gran decoro
Quanto ogn'altra autorevole persona.

A cavalier breathing as great a dignity
As any other person of authority.

The gravity and natural distinction of a man who had gone through the hard school of palace life are reflected in these lines. But what interested Boschini were the painter's personal opinions. And to make these agreeable to a Venetian, the Spaniard had no need to force himself. He passionately admired Tintoretto and extolled above all the *Glory* in the Ducal Palace, of which he was lucky enough to acquire a sketch, now in the Prado. Then Boschini put the inevitable question: "What about Raphael?" To this Velázquez replied with unabashed sincerity, admitting that he disliked him:

Rafael (a dire il vero,
Piasendome esser libero e sincero)
Stago perdir, che nol mi piase niente.

Raphael (truth to tell,
And I choose to be frank and sincere)
I was about to say I do not care for.

He made no secret of his views on art and the Venetian "reporter" thus set them down in verse:

A Venetia si trova el bon, e 'l belo
Mi, dago il primo luogo a quel penelo,
Tizian xe quel che porta la bandiera.

In Venice are the good and beautiful,
For my part I give first place to her painters,
And Titian is the standard-bearer.

So Velázquez, with the courage of his convictions, was not afraid to differ with orthodox opinions of Italian art. And he acted—that is to say he bought—accordingly. The pictures of Tintoretto, Veronese and Titian thus acquired by Velázquez are today the pride of the Prado. On his way to Naples he stopped in Rome, replenished his purse, and saw that the royal orders for works of art were properly filled. After seeing Ribera at Naples he returned to Rome and there met many artists: Bernini, Salvator Rosa, Pietro da Cortona. One wonders whether he may have met Poussin; the two men were so different temperamentally, one French, the other Spanish, one a rationalist, the other an existentialist, that they could hardly have taken to each other.

The reputation of Velázquez, his mission and the trust placed in him by the King of Spain, won him the great honor of painting the pope. Innocent X, of the Doria Pamphili family, offered a thankless subject for a painter anxious to idealize his model, but Velázquez was more than equal to the task. As the artist had been out of practice for the past year, he first made a trial portrait, to "warm up" his hand, of his servant Juan de Pareja. The portrait of Pareja won him a public triumph: exhibited in Rome at the Pantheon on March 19, 1650, it was more admired than any of the other works on view. Velázquez was elected a member of the Academy of St Luke, and then the pope sat to him. The result was a quickly, freely brushed portrait that spread his fame abroad. He declined any remuneration, and could only be prevailed on to accept a gold chain as a personal mark of esteem from the Holy Father. The pope's whole entourage insisted on having their portraits painted in turn: his sister-in-law Olimpia Maidalchini, who reigned over the papal court, Cardinal Astalli-Pamphili, the Monsignori of the chamber, and even the pope's barber. Velázquez also painted one of his colleagues, the woman painter Flaminia Trionfi. Except for the pope's and the cardinal's portraits, all these works have been lost.

He turned now to the errand on which he had come: the acquisition of statues and casts. Day after day he visited Roman collections and enjoyed to the full life in the papal city. But his king was growing impatient. He missed Velázquez and instructed his ambassadors to hasten his return. Velázquez had been due back in Madrid in June 1650. The Duke of L'Infantado, Spanish ambassador in Rome, received pointed orders from the king to arrange for the painter's return journey. "You know his phlegmatic nature," wrote Philip. "See that he does not take advantage of it to protract his sojourn at that court (i.e. in Rome)." But Velázquez was not to be hurried, and lingered on for another year. Five letters summoning him home were written by the king to his ambassador. The painter toyed with the idea of returning by way of Paris, but the wars then in progress made the journey hazardous and he had to give it up. In June 1651, a year behind schedule, he landed at Barcelona. He was never granted another leave of absence.

Work in abundance was waiting for him at the Alcázar. First came the exacting, unremitting task of painting portraits. In his absence a new queen had arrived at court; portraits had to be made of her and of the young Infanta, María Teresa, whose hand, when the time for marriage came, might be a diplomatic asset. Children were soon to be born to the ill-matched royal couple, and portraits of them had accordingly to be sent to foreign courts, as family presents, and to show that the future of the dynasty was assured. In the nine years left him to live, Velázquez produced a large body of work. He was awarded the highest honors and multiplied his titles to glory. It fell to him too, as to the curator of a museum in our day, to install the works of art he had brought back from Italy. The royal galleries could then boast of fabulous collections; those now in the Prado are only the remains. With the works for which no room could be found in the royal palace of Madrid, Velázquez organized another museum in the lower halls of the Escorial.

As time went on, the king looked upon him more and more as a trusted friend. When the post of Marshal of the Royal Household fell vacant in 1652, various candidates came forward and the council of high palace functionaries submitted its proposals to the king. No one placed the name of Velázquez at the head of the list of persons recommended; most of them added it at the end, a few gave it the next to last place; only one made bold to place it second. The king sent back the list with these words in the margin: "I appoint Velázquez." The post incurred heavy obligations and involved him in a maze of bureaucratic procedures: he had to take charge of the Privy Chamber, give orders, keep accounts, humor pride and vanity, and observe etiquette and precedence. His composure and self-possession enabled him to bear up under it all with philosophic detachment. He found relief from the petty vanities of the living in the silent friendship of the dead and the contemplation of their works. Titian, Tintoretto, Veronese, El Greco and Rubens, whose pictures hung in the galleries of the Alcázar, consoled him for the intrigues of his gilded prison. Sometimes he shut himself away in his studio, to commune with his own painting. And as always he found escape in nature, accompanying the king on his visits to the royal residences and on his hunting expeditions, beneath the shade trees of Aranjuez and the leafy vaults of the Pardo forest or the Valsain woods.

In 1658 the king took an even bolder step: he made Velázquez a Knight of Santiago, an inestimable title of nobility in that proud, caste-conscious society, exclusively preoccupied with prerogatives and privileges. Painters applauded, the aristocrats shook their heads. A dauber of canvases placed on an equal footing with the noblest Castilians! Still, it was not so easy to qualify. Velázquez' pedigree and estate had to be minutely inquired into by a royal commission; it had to be proved, and attested by witnesses, that his lineage was pure on both sides of the house, and furthermore that the exercise of painting had never been for him a mercenary profession. The salary he received from the king was discounted, for to serve his royal highness was an honor, not an employment; to the king he did not sell, he presented his pictures. The records of the commission contain the kindly, sometimes complaisant statements of aristocrats, knights of various orders, and friends of Velázquez' youth at Seville: Zurbarán, Alonso Cano, Nardi. The keeper of the royal records, Don Gaspar de Fuensalida, added that he "had always known him in the palace, in the king's service, as the greatest painter there was, and had ever been in Europe, according to the testimony of Rubens himself." To conclude the proceedings the pope's approbation was required. At length it came, and Velázquez was invested with the habit of the Order of Santiago in July 1659. He had but one year to live.

Honors and rank, yes, but how poor the reality behind them! A few months later we find the painter of the chamber and personal friend of the king claiming the arrears of his salary and informing the palace comptroller that the staff were being demoralized by the mismanagement of affairs: "Worst of all is this," he added, "that there is not a penny to be had to pay for the wood in the fireplaces of His Majesty's chamber." Disheartening penury, accounts behindhand, endless paperwork, spite and jealousy from courtiers, but confidence and friendship from the king, and an incomparable series of paintings—such is the strange and somber picture we get of Velázquez' last years.

It was left for him to shine in the ranks of the Spanish nobility on the last occasion on which the Austrian monarchy displayed, almost as its swan-song, the pomp of its solemn etiquette. The struggle between France and Spain for supremacy in Europe, two centuries old, was drawing to a close. Philip IV had sued for peace, and in 1659 was signed the treaty known to history as the Peace of the Pyrenees. To put the seal on it Philip consented to the marriage in the following year of his daughter María Teresa to Louis XIV of France, the rising star, the future Roi Soleil. The marriage ceremony took place in the Isle of Pheasants, in the Bidassoa, on the frontier of the two countries, in the presence of the two kings. As Marshal of the Royal Household, Velázquez preceded the king in order to see the living quarters prepared and the pavilions decorated. He left for Fuenterrabia on April 7, 1660. The state of his health must even then have been precarious, for, unusual with him, he travelled in a litter. The historic meeting of the kings took place. In order to provide a setting worthy of the occasion, Velázqucz had had the pavilions hung with the finest tapestries from the splendid royal collections. Moving among princes, ministers, grandees and great ladies, Velázquez performed his functions with tact and distinction.

Then, like an evil omen, the rumor spread in Madrid that he had died on the journey. When he reached home on June 26, the anxiety and distress of his family and friends were dispelled. But not for long. A hidden disorder combined with the fatigue of the journey had begun to tell on him. On July 31 the disease declared itself, sudden and violent. The king dispatched his own physicians, to no avail. On August 6, 1660, in the royal annex called the Casa del Tesoro, where he had painted his finest works, Velázquez died. The next day, escorted by a solemn procession of courtiers dressed in the habit of the order of knighthood to which he had lately been raised, the painter of Philip IV was interred in the church of St John the Baptist near the Alcázar. A few days later, faithful even to the rendezvous with death, Juana Pacheco was united to her husband in the tomb.

Of the king's grief we have a brief but eloquent testimony. Velázquez had been prevented by death from settling the accounts of his office. Bureaucratic routine takes no notice of mourning. Nine days after the painter's death a memorandum was submitted to the king calling for the reimbursement, in the State's favor, of fees received by Velázquez. Philip IV felt the indelicacy of this procedure. His thoughts turned to his deceased friend and, on the document that had revived his grief for the loss of so great a painter, he wrote these words which do him honor: "I am overwhelmed."

The life of Velázquez, with its background of artistic genius and its melancholy façade, unfolded like a dream within the walls of the royal palace. A clear, upright, unmysterious life as regards all the official, outward events referred to in the documents; but beyond that it is almost impossible to penetrate. Very seldom are we afforded a glimpse behind the closed door of his private life. What was he like in the integrity of his personality, in his inner reactions? Something of his character transpires in the few phrases he uttered which have come down to us; and reading between the lines, as best we can, of contemporary texts dealing with him, we may perhaps succeed in sketching out a picture of the man.

In his prentice years at Seville, Pacheco noted "his virtue, his rectitude, his happy penchants." "Good nature, noble blood," wrote Palomino. Andalusians are accounted resourceful, fickle, boastful. Velázquez was a staid, silent, serious-minded young man who went his own way, knew what he had to do, and did it. No hesitations, no influences. Steadfast, disconcerting self-confidence, with that aloofness shown by certain taciturn Andalusians. At the bottom of his soul Velázquez found his spiritual sustenance in his own superiority, but he never let this be felt by others, because his distinction of mind forbade him to do so. This superiority at once commanded the respect of his teacher, who acknowledged it in his book: "I do not esteem it discreditable that the pupil should surpass the master." Praiseworthy attitude for a man as possessed by his science and his learning as Pacheco was; it does honor to him as much as to his pupil. We know well enough that young painters in art schools readily undergo the influence of talented fellow students whose work announces the style of the day, and this explains the fact that the nascent fame of the prodigiously gifted adolescent who was painting "new things" quickly spread to all the studios in Seville. So it is that he very early came in contact with several apprentices who later became famous: Zurbarán and Alonso Cano, whose lifelong friend he remained. One hesitates to imagine him a gay and sociable comrade. Yet the imprint of the Sevillian genius seldom fails to make itself felt even in the gravest sons of that city. And that imprint is stamped on the rare, pithy, pertinent phrases from Velázquez' mouth which have been preserved. In Madrid he was nicknamed "El Sevillano." He never lost the delicate accent of his native province in his manner of speaking Castilian. One of his autograph signatures shows that he used the Andalusian *s* instead of the Castilian *z*, a slip still common today among natives of Andalusia.

At twenty-four he left his provincial studio for the Alcázar of the king of Spain, where he spent the rest of his life. What a difficult test this change was, and what a feather in the cap of a vain man so precocious a success might have been. But his equanimity, his nobility of character, preserved Velázquez from these dangers. He retained his self-possession and peace of mind, showed no surprise at his good fortune and took life as it came. Not only the known facts of his career make this clear, but also his work. He breathed the sweet incense of glory without losing his head. His lucid mind and powers of observation very soon enabled him, on the contrary, to see through the web of intrigue and scheming that generally distinguishes a court. And what a court! Turn to the literature of the period: Quevedo lashes at a Madrid of time-servers, petitioners, unsalaried soldiers, schemers, adventurers back from America, haughty nobles, and a whole rout of superstitious, picaresque hangers-on living on their wits and fawning on grandees.

An idle king stood somewhere far above them, like a myth, and it was given to very, very few to reach him. He sympathized at once with his young painter. He treated him with affection, esteem, friendliness, and admired him. This was too much for the envious, pretentious, mediocre painters of the court, who would have none of him. Carducho's *Diálogos* are full of anonymous pin-pricks aimed at the newcomer: the great painters had never been portraitists; the important thing was not sleight of hand, but imagination and abidance by an ideal composition; the secret of art lay not in color, but in design; the painter who contents himself with the natural was like the play-actor who recites lines written by others; imitation was mere empiricism; painting could be good even if ill-colored, and so on. Velázquez must have been for Carducho "that monster of dexterity and naturalness," devoid of precepts and doctrine, to whom he alludes in his book. The ideal, the doctrine, for this the old mannerist yearned with academic nostalgia. The disregard of principles in the new manner of painting would, he foretold, prove to be the ruin of art, whose doom was already presaged in still lifes of abject meanness and low-mindedness, and in pictures of topers and good-for-nothings. Here was a direct attack. Proof again that there is nothing new under the sun; these pessimistic lamentations have broken out anew at each stylistic crisis in art history.

Velázquez went his way undeterred, reasserting his self-confidence in terse rejoinders, as always a man of few words. He would rather, he said, be first in his rough manner than second in an affected mannerism. One day, the king having said to him, "They claim that heads are the only thing you know how to paint," he replied, "This is a great honor, Sire, for hitherto I have never seen a head well painted." In Italy he expressed his opinion of Raphael with the same frankness with which El Greco told Pacheco in Toledo that Michelangelo was a good fellow, but unfortunately did not know how to paint.

Ortega y Gasset has singled out and emphasized Velázquez' aspiration to the nobility, which he considered the key to his character. Even while making due allowance for the prejudices of the age, I cannot believe that the mainspring of his career is to be sought for in such an ambition. Velázquez, as Boschini acknowledges, was a man of noble nature, noble bearing, noble manners. His reserve tinged with aloofness, his uneffusive generosity and warm, unostentatious kindness won him, in spite of the enmity a superior man is bound to arouse, the sincere attachment of many excellent friends. Witness the fifty-nine persons of quality who testified in his favor during the inquiry preceding his nomination to the Order of Santiago. Even when he had reached the highest offices, the petty vexations of his colleagues and of the palace administration failed to touch him. He knew nothing of adulation, backbiting, intrigue. The man who painted those landscapes of blue mountains bathed in gray light could only have been a contemplative spirit, a lover of solitude, shut in the world of his own meditations. The king's esteem sustained him. Philip IV liked to repair to his studio and watch him paint; and a chair was at all times reserved there for him. Through the windows of the gallery of the Cierzo (north wind) streamed the pure light of the Castilian plateau, and the sun that tempered its cold winters and went down in splendor. In those quiet hours at his easel, how could Velázquez have been otherwise than happy! His vision was so keen that, as soon as he had laid in the essential, he lost any concern with putting a smooth finish on the picture. He worked at his own rhythm, quite dispassionately, with an elegant economy of means, as Andalusians generally do. Then he left his studio for the business of the antechamber: accounts, reports and memoranda from the keeper of the records and the comptroller, surveillance of work in progress, and tedious minutiae. The most congenial of his duties was no doubt the fitting up of the king's new residences, the hanging of pictures by the great masters which had to harmonize with the decorations, had to balance and complement each other. Here a golden-tinted Titian, there a green-flushed Tintoretto; a little further on, opulent nudes by Rubens; in a ceremonial hall, portraits by Moro and Coello. An idea of the refinement of his taste may be had from an incidental remark of Palomino, who describes the care with which Velázquez chose his costume for the solemn meeting of the Infanta and Louis XIV: "As for the color of the cloth, one had to admire how well it suited him, for he was superior in his knowledge of materials and always showed great taste in choosing them."

Of his private life we know nothing more. A quiet home, a loving wife, a married daughter whose children brightened the house. A son-in-law who was at once a disciple and assistant. An uneventful, unadventurous artist's life, unattended by anecdote or eccentricity, but answering to a profound sense of serenity and peace. The confessions of Velázquez are in his works. Praising one of his pictures, a poet of the day coined this apt expression: "The soul breathes out through his brush."

A noble soul, a proud spirit. Thus Velázquez appears to us.

The Infanta Margarita (detail), 1659-1660. Prado, Madrid.

LIFE FIRST OF ALL

"And because your perfections, Lord, were infinite, and a single creature could not embody them all, it was necessary to create many in order for each, for its part, piecemeal, to reveal something of all."

FRAY LUIS DE GRANADA.

F EW painters have been as impervious as Velázquez to what are called influences. For a young artist beginning his career it is difficult indeed to escape the environment in which he and his masters were schooled. But from the outset Velázquez drew on his own resources. He broke radically with what was current practice in the studios of his day. The painters of Seville were then producing enormous altar pictures, whose composition was heavy and redundant, whose figures were conventional; these works purported to echo the grandiose monumentality of the Italian painters, but were in reality no more than a naive and clumsy reflection of them.

This was provincial art, with a certain bravura of handling in the work of Herrera, with brilliant color effects in that of Roelas. None of this could have any interest for Velázquez, except when temperament broke through convention. Herrera the Elder, for example, showed flashes of a new painting; hence the importance of Velázquez' brief apprenticeship in his studio. Herrera was a vehement, short-tempered man, and a harsh taskmaster, and if Palomino is to be believed, his pupils could never bear with him very long. From the same author we learn that Velázquez stayed but a short time, which indicates his precocity, for he was only eleven when he entered Pacheco's studio. With his bold brushwork, his rich impasto, his sober palette and ochre tonalities, Herrera undoubtedly had some weight in the formation of Velázquez. At the very least, he must be given credit for feeling and responding to the imperative of his time, its "need of prose," and so he abandoned now and then the "great machines" of his religious works for still lifes which deserved the renown they won.

When Velázquez began to make a name for himself with his still lifes, Herrera must have claimed the honor of having shown him the way. Pacheco's jealousy was aroused and, without naming Herrera, he waxes indignant in his book that anyone else should dare to arrogate that glory to himself. The point at issue would be unimportant, were we not bound to acknowledge that Velázquez' early works, his delineations of kitchens and studies from life, are closer to Herrera than to Pacheco, whose re-echoes of Michelangelo savored too much of theory to be anything but discouraging to a young painter.

Unconsciously, but resolutely, the apprentice turned away from those vast, futile compositions, which today fill the largest rooms in the Seville museum; he insisted on reinserting painting in the only element that attracted him—in immersing it, that is, in the current of life. This he resolved to do. In view of this new approach to painting, it matters little whether or not in his youth Velázquez saw any pictures by Caravaggio. The latter, in spite of his overwrought gesticulations, his violent light effects and all the stock devices of Baroque composition which he used, is indeed, as Zahn has said, "the last of the classics." The first fruits of Velázquez' art, and even more the guiding purpose which led him to paint as he did, were very different.

The few details Pacheco gives us of his pupil's ways show how independent he was of his master, and how surprised the latter was at his tastes. "While still a child," writes Pacheco, "he used to pay a little peasant to serve him as a model in different postures and actions, crying or laughing, without shirking any difficulty." This means that the copying of classical models from prints held little or no interest for him. He found life itself more appealing, the forms of objects, the qualities of color, everything we perceive visually, whose marrow has to be extracted to make a work of art. Beauty, for him, was not a disembodied ideal but the concrete reality of existence; if, from that raw material, an artist can distil the quintessence, he will succeed in making a work of art, for beauty consists not in juxtaposing natural forms around an idea artificially inspired by the complacent admiration of antiquity, but in

An Old Woman Frying Eggs, 1618. National Gallery of Scotland, Edinburgh.

working out an expressive, sensuous figuration grounded in reality. What we thus define in an *a posteriori* synthesis was for Velázquez purely a matter of lucid intuition. Life itself, unalloyed with the stuff of dreams or phantasmagoria, was the first term and condition of success. This was Velázquez' self-imposed point of departure in his simple and modest acceptance of reality: objects and persons, first of all, uncompromisingly and truthfully represented. This was not the end but the means to an end.

The painter opened his eyes on what was in front of him: a peasant, his model, or a kitchen-maid. In the foreground, a table whose nuances and shadows the studio light enabled him to capture, and on which objects stood out singly in all the sharpness of their form and texture. The dull glow of earthenware, the golden crust of bread, the transparency of glasses, the downy skin of fruit, the flickering gleams of copper, what modest wonders! Giving himself up to the delineation of them, as if training himself to record real, tangible life at close range, Velázquez, a nominalist without realizing it, discovered the visual

An Old Woman Frying Eggs
(detail), 1618.
National Gallery of Scotland,
Edinburgh.

An Old Woman Frying Eggs (detail), 1618. National Gallery of Scotland, Edinburgh.

beauty of the world. It is true that, generally speaking, the Baroque age took an interest in the theme of still life, lending itself as it does to displays of technical wizardry and color effects. But how different are Velázquez' interiors in conception and pictorial quality from the virtuoso execution and gaudy butcher's stalls of the Flemings and Italians! What Velázquez painted in this line remains, rather, within the sober, austere tradition, intimate and concentrated, of Fray Juan Sánchez Cotan, the painter of Toledo whose still lifes are so steeped in poetry and humility, in an accentuated chiaroscuro, and who was active around 1600, at a time when the innovations of Caravaggio were as yet unknown in Spain.

The Kitchen Maid, with Christ at Emmaus, c. 1620. National Gallery of Ireland, Dublin.

Chance, as a rule, is responsible for the anthology of a given body of work bequeathed to us by the past. If we assume that a painter's logical evolution—reality, however, is not necessarily logical—is from the simple to the complex, then we should consider Velázquez' earliest Sevillian works to be those which appear least crowded and which are treated as studies rather than finished pictures. Into this category would come the two versions of *The Kitchen Maid* (Art Institute of Chicago and National Gallery of Ireland, Dublin) and the *Two Young Men at Table* (Apsley House, London). On the other hand, and this too carries weight in establishing a chronology, the two versions of *Peasants at Table* (Budapest and Leningrad) are the pictures which seem to come closest to the painting of Herrera the Elder. These are the most naive and variegated of his works, and on this account may be regarded as the earliest in date. The two versions of *The Kitchen Maid* and the pictures immediately following them already evince the serenity and peace which were soon to characterize the whole of his work; they are truly imbued with the painter's spirit. "He liked to drill himself in studying the expressions of the human face," Pacheco tells us. Taking this as a touchstone, the first pictures in which laughing figures appear, caught in lively, unguarded attitudes, might be held to be the earliest works, as this anecdotal attitudinizing was soon to give way to gravity and reserve.

Musical Trio ("Los Musicos"), c. 1620. Staatliche Museen, Berlin.

Kitchen Scene with Christ in the House of Martha and Mary, 1619-1620.
National Gallery, London.

The two pictures of *Peasants at Table* mentioned above and the *Vintager* from the O.B. Cintas Collection, New York (if this is really by Velázquez), would show him entering on the path he followed after the *Kitchen Maids*. The *Musical Trio* in Berlin stands out among Velázquez' early works owing to a more plastic execution, polished forms, volumes dry and stiff as cardboard, and the presence of elements which may be considered Caravaggesque. But except for the smiling boy and the table in perspective, the folded napkins, the boy's hand in the immediate foreground, the nodding of heads, and the bend of the arm holding the violin are already features peculiar to Velázquez.

The cleaning of the Dublin *Kitchen Maid* has revealed a distant representation of Christ at Emmaus in the upper lefthand corner. The same device occurs in the more mature painting of *Christ in the House of Martha and Mary* (National Gallery, London). Whether this is meant to be an actual scene glimpsed outside the room or a painted picture hung on the wall is not clear. The ambiguity is intentional on Velázquez' part. It conveys his aloofness from the theme, a certain bashfulness before the religious subject, for fear perhaps of lapsing into conventional rhetoric and so departing from life. There can be no doubt that the girl with mortar and pestle in *Christ in the House of Martha and Mary* is the same as the one portrayed in another scene, simpler in composition (*Girl at Table*, Maric Collection, Santa Monica, California), which must be numbered among Velázquez' very earliest works. The transition toward this deepening insight into visible reality is to be found, I think, in the *Old Woman Frying Eggs* (National Gallery of Scotland, Edinburgh).

The most momentous innovation of all these pictures lies in the intensification of certain presences, rendered immediately perceptible by the abnormal disposition of the foreground seen from above. The cinema has accustomed our eyes to a heightening of expressive values in the foreground. This shift of emphasis, which Velázquez discovered while still a youth, is both physical and psychic. Seen from this angle, which is not that of either ordinary or academic vision, things acquire a force which compensates for the humble purposes they usually serve. Here was a radical novelty: the simplest objects of daily life, valued by the painter for their qualities of form and texture, move into the foreground while all the rest becomes secondary, including the religious theme, in some pictures a mere allusion. Eggs frying in oil, or a large earthenware jar distorted by high perspective, these become the center of focus and, in Velázquez' hands, rise to the top of the hierarchy of picture elements. There had been nothing like this even in Caravaggio, and at the sight of this innovation the academic painters of the day, who considered still life to be the lowest, most vulgar form of painting, could only brand it as an aberration.

Velázquez rose in quick stages toward the mastery of his art. He achieved it to the full in the *Water Carrier of Seville*. Here his intention was consciously carried out, and the stage of the "nature piece" is superseded in this flawless composition, which contains much more than mere appearances. The point is that Velázquez always disdains anecdote and goes straight to the painting. His canvas is first of all a play of volumes whose fully rounded plasticity delights him: a jug in the very forefront, a jar, and a glass of transparent crystal; then curved forms caressed by the eye and the brush, with the diagonal rhythm of three heads set off against the penumbra; lastly, a barely inflected diagonal, formed by the fold of the leading figure's smock, subdues the rhythm of volumes and curves. The humanization and unruffled peace of this work

The Water Carrier of Seville, 1618-1620.
Wellington Museum,
Apsley House, London.

The Water Carrier of Seville (detail), 1618-1620.
Collection of Count Contini-Bonacossi, Florence.

37

come to bear on this point, slightly off-center, on which attention is focused: the meeting of hands and glass which introduces something almost ritual into this trivial scene. The judicious color scheme is in no way inferior. Two bright notes descend along a diagonal, the water carrier's sleeve and the boy's collar, while a whole scale of earth colors is orchestrated in the penumbra.

Parallel with this production, Velázquez had to pursue a necessary and not overly enthusiastic initiation into religious painting. His *Immaculate Virgin* and *St John the Baptist*, both treated as hard volumes, in dark flesh tints, are like figures carved in wood. The *Supper at Emmaus* in New York offers a characteristic alliance of a pious subject and a popular atmosphere. The animation of the apostles' gestures comes as a surprise, even though it is called for by the theme. The picture has suffered a good deal, but I believe it to be by Velázquez' hand and I know for a fact that copies of it existed at Seville. The *Adoration of the Magi* in the Prado is, to my mind, a maturer work because here his approach to the religious theme proceeds directly from life. From now on the artist confronts all the themes he sets out to paint, religious, mythological or historical, by freeing himself from the idealizing conventions of the Renaissance and Mannerist tradition, or better, as Ortega y Gasset put it, by "reducing the subject to its logarithm of reality." In the case of the Prado *Adoration*, the theme becomes more accessible because reduced in effect to the theme of a family picture. The work is signed and I believe the date should be read as 1619. In that year, having recently married, Velázquez had a daughter. The birth of the child, the woman penetrated with her motherhood, the homage paid by the onlookers, the miracle wrought afresh by each new appearance of life, all this is in the picture and also arose at that time out of the personal experience of Velázquez himself. The tonality is yellowish brown, but carmines and pale greens begin to appear, indicating an enrichment of his palette. Whether or not he took his wife as a model, Velázquez saw the Virgin through Juana de Miranda, and Jesus beneath the features of the child born, or about to be born, to him. Models also appear in this picture who

The Adoration of the Magi, 1619. Prado, Madrid.

recur in all his work of this period. The composition presents the same pattern of organization: a crossing of diagonals. Its center of focus is the marvellous head of the Child, quivering with life. Patches of light and shade are balanced intentionally and not allowed to alter the forms of figures arbitrarily. Channelled by the light, attention is brought to bear on the group of Mother and Child and centered on the essential point, which gives its significance to the picture: the hand of the kneeling king offering his gifts. Here skill is seconded by the painter's instinct and not by the academic precedents revered by his teacher.

Referring to the discipline Velázquez imposed on himself in the study of nature, Pacheco says that in this way he "achieved sureness in

Portrait of the Poet Luis de Góngora, 1622. Museum of Fine Arts, Boston.

St Ildefonso Receiving the Chasuble from the Virgin (detail), 1623.
Museo Provincial de Bellas Artes, Seville.

portraiture." And it is true that Velázquez was passionately attracted by the thing that stood in front of him, whether being or object, man or jar. How could he help being attracted by portraits too? The ones he painted while still at Seville have the same pictorial force, the same clean-cut plasticity, the same yellowish brown tonality as his still lifes and religious pictures. Such are the portrait of Cristóbal Suárez de Ribera with, for the first time, a lyrical glimpse of a landscape; the head in the Prado supposed to represent Pacheco; and above all the impressive effigy in the Prado of the nun of Toledo who, at sixty-five, wasted and wrinkled by so many years of enclosure, sailed from Seville to found a convent at Manila. All these works, together with a sequence of apostles of which a few are extant, must have been painted before 1622, when Velázquez

St Ildefonso Receiving the Chasuble from the Virgin, 1623.
Museo Provincial de Bellas Artes, Seville.

paid his first visit to Madrid. The portrait of Góngora (Boston Museum), executed then, links up directly with the earlier portraits. The nun and the poet are alike in their tremendous energy. Velázquez plumbs the model and reveals its character to us with impressive force, the force of life itself.

What a breath of novelty stirs too in the strange picture of *St Ildefonso Receiving the Chasuble from the Virgin* (Seville). This is a resolute and at the same time almost too naive attempt to express the allusion to a supernatural world. The solution adopted is unusual in the School of Seville, hitherto accustomed to treat the subject on a large scale and to leave a respectable distance between heaven and earth. This is only hinted at here by a few solid gray clouds which barely rise above the ground on which the saint is kneeling. I am inclined to believe that this picture was painted after his first visit to Madrid and his first sight of paintings by El Greco, whose clouds have some similarity with those painted by Velázquez, but here the resemblance ends. The Virgin and her companions inhabiting these unusual clouds are also taken from life; they are, quite literally, girls of Seville, as their features and coiffure make plain. The only thing missing is a flower in their hair. Yet this ingenuous picture is by no means trivial. Its force of execution saves it from lapsing into anecdote and Velázquez' method asserts its authority: a total concentration on the reality of the saint's head—light and life —and on the feminine hands which grant him their gift.

The youthful stage of Velázquez' work thus draws to a close. An almost magical change was about to come over the artist's life. But in the process of adapting himself to the new tasks awaiting him in a very different milieu, it is safe to say that he found it greatly to his advantage now to have repudiated, from the very first, the Mannerist ambience and academic convention. To find his authentic and original expression, he had thus been free at the outset to go straight to life. And this harsh and passionate contact henceforth enabled him, without surrendering anything of himself, to approach kings and freaks, great captains and adventurers, infantas and gods, with the same freedom.

King Philip IV in Full Length, c. 1628. Prado, Madrid.

PAINTER TO THE KING

"We painters, however lowly our station may be, are yet able to confer a favor even on kings."

PALOMINO.

WHEN Fonseca summoned Velázquez to a court dominated by the influence of Olivares, the painter's life took a decisive turn. The shy provincial suddenly found himself, at twenty-four, moving among the high and mighty of the earth. A fairy's wand touched Velázquez' head and the world changed from what it was. The king at once fell under the spell of this young man, nearly of his own age, who was master of so prodigious an art. It was a stroke of luck for Velázquez that, with Antonio Moro, Sánchez Coello and Pantoja de la Cruz, the Spanish court had grown accustomed to a severe style of portraiture devoid of mundane pomp and courtly flattery. For the genuine Spaniard, man comes before social hierarchies, before power or money—flesh-and-blood man, who lives, says Unamuno, on the hunger of immortality. For him, over and above any functions, any social role or duties, stands the human person; and this is the greatness and the limitation of his condition as a Spaniard. As Américo Castro has said, the integrity of the human person is the essential value for this hard and ascetic people, accustomed to glory and poverty, to exaltation and renunciation.

Neither the first effigy Velázquez painted of his king nor the equestrian portrait exhibited in 1625 on the steps of the monastery of San Felipe has been preserved. His earliest extant court portraits are those of Philip IV (Metropolitan Museum, New York) and Olivares (São Paulo Museum), both painted in 1624 to the order of Doña Antonia Ipeñarrieta; the receipts of her payments signed by Velázquez himself still exist, and thus ironically belie the obliging statements of the painter's friends who, when the king nominated him to the Order of

Santiago, testified on oath that Velázquez had never taken money for his pictures (this was the condition of his elevation to the knighthood).

The authenticity of these two portraits has been challenged, but I believe groundlessly; both are well documented. In 1624, moreover, the artist could scarcely have had any disciples in Madrid familiar with his manner and capable of producing such perfect replicas. One cannot help noticing that in these portraits Velázquez was experiencing some difficulty in adapting himself to his new tasks. He failed as yet to dominate the silhouette and did not pose the figure as he was soon to do. Indeed, with the full-length portrait of Philip IV in the Prado and thereafter, we find him making rapid progress, visible notably in the correction of the awkward, compass-like arrangement of the legs. This is one of the first examples of Velázquez' famous pentimenti. The silhouette, the gesture, the grasp of the personage, and the composition are even more successful in the portraits of Olivares (Hispanic Society, New York), dating to 1625. Then, in the portrait of the Infante Don Carlos, the painter at one bound equalled the masters of aristocratic distinction in the male portrait—Titian, Van Dyck, the English. But there is no affectation in the elegance, it is compounded of nobility, ease, gravity, humanity, and also an indefinable natural grace. The model's inimitable way of holding his hat and dangling an empty glove from his finger-tips are two lucky finds. The invention goes well beyond realism or naturalism, it reveals the painter's determination to work out an unrhetorical style of his own.

Ochres now disappeared, and with his blacks Velázquez composed an orchestration of nuances such as only a great colorist is capable of. Though in the model's face linger traces of the strong plasticity of his Seville period, in the silhouette and play of values Velázquez has already met his problem: man in his surrounding atmosphere. Anecdote is absent; there is no furniture in the room, the figure stands alone, solitary as an apparition, like "something that looms into sight," as Ortega y Gasset aptly observed. Velázquez attenuated the outlines with a brush that freed the silhouette of any linear dryness. The model thus

The Infante Don Carlos in Full Length, c. 1626. Prado, Madrid.

emerges enveloped in air, surrounded by a fluidity that moves with his figure and situates him in space. So it is that the references to a measured space are kept to a minimum. A mere brushstroke suffices to indicate the angle of intersection between floor and wall; later even this slight reference disappeared. Of this portrait, which already contains the whole of Velázquez, Beruete writes: "It is impossible to meet with a painting more alive, more perfect in its simplicity; nature is taken unawares by the synthetic vision of Velázquez and interpreted by him with innate superiority."

Thus the glory of the portraitist was already firmly established. But was Velázquez merely a portraitist? Nothing more than that, murmured the envious. The king resolved to put him to the test in a large composition. This was the *Expulsion of the Moriscoes* of 1627, now lost, which gave him his first chance of tackling a historical picture. Shortly afterwards he painted the *Triumph of Bacchus*, whose "logarithm of reality" found apt expression in its popular title: *The Topers*. Velázquez still stood in need of passive and patient sitters of character, such as would enable him to train his eye and pursue his investigation of life, for his brush remained obsessed, as it were, with the representation of life's irreducible singularities, as is proved by his first pictures of court jesters, which date from this period. *The Topers*, though it falls in line with his Sevillian works, denotes a higher ambition and raises a major problem: the anti-rhetorician Velázquez confronts mythology. He had already become acquainted with the great Italian masters, in the matchless gallery of the Alcázar in Madrid, and also with Rubens, but had remained virtually uninfluenced by them. His devotees of the cult of Bacchus might have stepped from the pages of *Lazarillo de Tormes* or *Guzmán de Alfarache*, picaresque wine-bibbers grouped around a handsome, half-naked youth. This is prose without frivolity. *The Topers*, as Mayer has written, "have nothing in common with the coarse models used by Dutch painters." These are neither marionettes nor puppets; these are men. Once again appear the diagonal and the intersection of lines, the hands of light crowning the toper in the middle,

The Topers or The Triumph of Bacchus ("Los Borrachos"), detail, 1628. Prado, Madrid.

and the eye can follow the path of light traced out by the arm of this prosaic Bacchus. But Velázquez has made a further discovery: landscape. A concrete, spacious, grandiose landscape, which spreads out from the banks of the Manzanares. But this was only a tentative effort; his greatest conquests in landscape came later, as his pictorial language was broadened and deepened, when he stood in full possession of his abbreviated manner and succeeded in making us feel atmosphere.

The Topers or The Triumph of Bacchus ("Los Borrachos"), 1628. Prado, Madrid.

The destiny and fortune of Velázquez lay in the fact that, like Ribera, but with a vaster horizon, he was the only Spanish painter of his generation—the decisive generation of Spanish painting—who eluded isolation and provincialism. It was also his good fortune to enjoy the friendship of Rubens during the eight months the Flemish master spent in Madrid (1628-1629). Then there was his journey to Italy (1629-1631). This came as the complement of friendly relations maintained daily with the works of the great Italian masters in the Alcázar. Velázquez travelled

Apollo in Vulcan's Forge, 1630. Prado, Madrid.

to see and learn, and worked little abroad. But the two pictures he did paint in Rome owe something to Italy. His conception remains personal, and his differences from the Italian painters exceed his debt to them. In *Vulcan's Forge* Apollo informs Vulcan of the infidelity of Venus. There is no gesturing; the scandalous news makes the men pause in their work and centers their attention on the visitor. This restraint, charged with intensity, is the reverse of Caravaggio's frantic gesticulation, and equally far removed from the expressive urbanity of

Joseph's Bloodstained Coat Brought to Jacob, 1630. Chapter House, Escorial.

the Venetians or Guercino. More akin to the latter is *Joseph's Coat* (Escorial), although, as was the Spanish painter's way, the interest is again centered on the lozenge formed by the arms and hands of the two figures holding the bloodstained coat. The diagonal is emphasized; planes of light and shadow divide the picture in a carefully weighed proportion. The feeling for color and the lighting are very different from Guercino's lunar clarity. Already, behind the two figures coming up in the background, there appears that screen of penumbra which Velázquez introduced to mark his investigations of space. The glimpse of a landscape denotes his awakening sense of a new vocation.

Another exceptional group of religious pictures dates from after his return from Italy in 1631. *Christ at the Column* (National Gallery, London) and *Christ on the Cross* (Prado) point to a growing interest in the nude which was certainly the result of this journey. But even in the most academic of his works, the London *Christ*, the pulse of life beats in the delightful figure of the little girl. The Prado *Christ* is an example of reserve and serenity rare in Christian iconography. This is a dead Christ depicted without emotionalism, at once real and distant. This painting inspired Unamuno to write a poem expressive of a profound religious sentiment aspiring to faith. The picture at Orihuela, the *Temptation of St Thomas Aquinas*, also has a fitness and restraint in contrast with the frenzied expression characteristic of his time. The composition rich in interior space, the variations of lighting, the still life elements, all are highly personal. As usual, the intense and sober expression is concentrated on the hands. Those of the angel are a matchless example of delicacy and sensibility.

This group of pictures, except for the Prado *Christ*, painted with bitumens which have sometimes led to the assumption that the work pre-dates his journey to Italy, vouch for the progress Velázquez was making in the handling of his medium. The palette is brighter and the execution freer, color being applied in light coats which, as with the Venetians, allow the grain of the canvas to show through. In the heads of the two pictures of *Vulcan's Forge* and *Joseph's Coat*, the simplification of technique, the scumbles and accents are a prodigy of accuracy. To fathom the secret of life Velázquez no longer needed to resort to the violent intensity of his Seville paintings; from now on his arms were lightness, allusiveness, economy of means. He was the contrary of a virtuoso.

Philip IV on Horseback, c. 1635. Prado, Madrid.

THE GLORIES OF BUEN RETIRO

"His painting divine,
Silent poem, mute history,
Enthrals our senses
And reigns over memory."
                MANUEL GALLEGOS,
Silva topográfica del Buen Retiro, 1637.

A great task was waiting for Velázquez at the royal palace when he took up his brushes again after his return from Italy (1631). In view of his unremitting, unerring investigation of life, it must have seemed as if he intended to reduce the whole of painting to the portrait of life. Weary of an idealized archetype, like that of Raphael or of Michelangelo, he felt within him the growing need to paint *individuals*. Now the artist hearkened to the call of things, he fell back on the poetry of life and discovered the mystery of unique experience, which can never repeat itself.

The trivial delineation of everyday life as we find it in the naturalism of the nineteenth century, in the so-called "nature piece," is something altogether different. With Velázquez, painting probed into one of the world's gravest mysteries—the mystery alluded to by philosophers when they speak of the *principium individuationis*. The naturalism of the nineteenth century was only a neo-style. Velázquez' realism is imbued with a will to transcendence. It answers to a Spanish vision of the world, aptly illustrated by the text of Fray Luis de Granada inscribed at the head of the second chapter of this volume. There is a book by Cardinal Bellarmine entitled *On the Knowledge of God through his Creatures*. This might be taken as the leitmotiv of Velázquez' art. To the Spanish mind, God resides not in the kind of intellectual club made up by the world of Platonic ideas, but reveals himself to us in the humblest realities. Human values derive from the mere fact of existing; and not from faith, duty, or the sense of a social mission, nor from intelligence or power. At bottom, for a Spaniard, all men are truly equal, and it is for art to reflect this profound awareness of individualization, for the individual is transient and variable, as far as the matter goes of which he is made; but he is the truth as postulated for us not only by our intelligence but by our vital reason. Truth is existence and existence is history, and history too pursues truth. Cervantes has well expressed this in an often-quoted passage: "Because History is something sacred, it must be truthful; wheresoever is truth, there is God, truth being an aspect of the Godhead." To the humanist mind of the Renaissance, truth and art were opposed to each other. Velázquez set out in his painting to show the falsity of this alleged opposition. Lope de Vega agreed with him, and in his comedy *Lo fingido verdadero* he sums up his aesthetic credo in these lines:

"For those who cling to the rules of art
Will never of true nature show any part."

Velázquez is the highest example of one of those moments, rarer than is commonly supposed in the history of art, which witness the triumph of what has been called in another field "the aesthetic of the individual's salvation"; and this aesthetic, in spite of momentary eclipses, was better suited than any other to the Spanish vocation in the great age of the seventeenth century. But let it not be forgotten that the Spaniard, being an extremist, is always ready to leap without transition to the opposite extreme. Witness Picasso and Miró, who in a way are no less Spanish than Velázquez.

Velázquez then lived through a few years of optimism at the Spanish court. A deceptive optimism it proved to be, a giddy sense of well-being trumped up and sustained by the dictator Olivares to flatter his monarch. And dictators, when they leave off telling their usual lies, either ignore or are blind to the truth. The favorite endeavored to create around his master an atmosphere of power and victory. The king spent his time in an idle succession of hunting expeditions, country pleasures and merry-making, performances of comedies and recitations of poetry, love affairs with women of low birth, and the favorite exploited the king's tendency to neglect the business of government. The palace of

Buen Retiro with its architecture and its gardens, due to the personal initiative of Olivares, remains the symbol of these years of counterfeit glory, when in reality the Spanish power lay on the brink of ruin and the empire was slowly falling apart. In 1631, at the first entertainment given at Buen Retiro, a comedy was performed with this symbolic title: "He who lies most will grow greatest." Here is a fitting motto for the dictatorships of all periods. In 1632 Olivares presented the king with the key to the new palace. The works to adorn it soon followed; he was then busying himself with the decoration of the main rooms. The heart of the

Philip IV Hunting Wild Boar in the Pardo, c. 1638. National Gallery, London.

The Count-Duke of Olivares on Horseback, c. 1638. Prado, Madrid.

palace was the so-called Salón de los Reinos. There, with a series of historical pictures, the minister planned to immortalize the victorious feats of arms which seemed to augur so well for the reign of Philip IV: victories won in the Low Countries, in Germany, in America, against the Dutch, against the coalitions at the start of the Thirty Years' War, against the English too. Velázquez was accordingly commissioned to represent the surrender of Breda, in the Netherlands, at the end of a long siege, during which the town was defended by Justin of Nassau, while the victorious army was led by the noble and accomplished Genoese general Ambrosio Spinola.

This is unquestionably the finest historical picture of European painting. Avoiding any suggestion of the rhetorical or pompous, Velázquez infused his work with his own courtesy and humanity. He represents, in the simplest way, the meeting of the two generals, at the moment the town capitulates. Spinola, an exemplary type of aristocratic amenity, bows with a smile toward his adversary and, with a scarcely perceptible gesture, spares him the humiliation of kneeling before the victor. Here are two antagonists who have played a fair game, and who may continue to be considered as two knights and gentlemen. A supreme lesson in good breeding and humanity which our time, with its pride in technical progress and science, has forgotten. Velázquez composes his picture with flawless skill and great sobriety. The cross-pattern receding in depth in the form of an *X* serves to focus attention on the central group, through a play of curves beginning in the foreground with the Dutch soldier seen from behind and the rump of the Spanish general's horse. The center of the picture and the gist of its meaning are marked by Nassau's outstretched hand, presenting the victor with the key to the city. A vast landscape of flooded fields creates distance and atmosphere; the fires of Breda cloud the horizon with smoke. Velázquez' palette is richer and brighter than ever before; his composition is a find full of happy invention. Obstinate investigators of sources and influences have sought at all costs to point out antecedents of Velázquez' originality, but they cannot detract from his merit.

Ortega y Gasset noted with his keen irony: "No sooner does a picture with a lance in the air turn up than we are asked to regard it as a precedent of the one by Velázquez. Looking closely at these precursors, it will be seen that much more genius would have been needed to dissociate this element of lances from their pictures and give it the role it plays in the *Surrender of Breda* than to invent everything *ex nihilo*." But unfortunately the specialists in art history, on the lookout for anything that will yield a magazine article or a paper for an art-historical congress, prefer to linger over the short-sighted, comparative analysis of photographs, instead of seeking to cultivate the enjoyment of works of art or to elicit their aesthetic and historical significance.

The Lances, finished before 1635, stands out as the major achievement of this period. Yet his work as a portraitist is no less fine. The beautiful queen Isabelle de Bourbon did not like to pose, and this explains the mediocre quality of most of the portraits of her which have been preserved. Velázquez, passionately fond of the natural and vital, must have been able to do no more than lay in a few brushstrokes whenever the opportunity arose. To execute the large canvases ordered from him, he probably disposed only of a head painted from the model. Hence the suspicion that the extant portraits are only studio works. But two full-length portraits of the queen, with their fine colors, stand out from this middling production: one in the Copenhagen museum and another in an English collection. The pendant of this prototype may be the portrait of *Philip IV in Brown and Silver* in the National Gallery, London. What a distance separates this from the severe effigies of the previous decade! The dark dress and the ruff have been replaced by a rich costume which brings into play the full resources of Velázquez' sumptuous palette, with its carmines beautifully setting off the king's golden hair, leather hat, gloves and plumes.

Large equestrian portraits of the royal family were ordered to embellish the palace of Buen Retiro. There are five of these. In three of them—those of Philip III, Queen Margarita, and Isabelle de Bourbon —Velázquez shared the work with others. The last-named portrait is a

The Surrender of Breda ("Las Lanzas"), 1634-1635. Prado, Madrid.

Philip IV in Brown and Silver, c. 1635. National Gallery, London.

striking demonstration of the difference between Velázquez and his collaborators. The head of the queen and the horse are two superb pieces of painting, because here again Velázquez penetrated life, whereas those who painted the clothes and the backgrounds of the pictures were only mediocre imitators whose artless efforts were rendered insipid by their incapacity. Who were Velázquez' helpers? At that festive period the king's painter was surrounded by colleagues, painters of stage scenery, and decorators. Already collaborating with him was his faithful disciple and zealous imitator Juan Bautista del Mazo, who in 1634 had married his daughter Francisca. The two equestrian portraits entirely by the hand of Velázquez, that of Philip IV on a rearing horse and that of Prince Don Baltasar Carlos on his spirited young mare, are outstanding works,

Prince Don Baltasar Carlos
on Horseback, c. 1635.
Prado, Madrid.

The Cardinal Infante
Don Fernando as a Huntsman, c. 1636.
Prado, Madrid.

especially the latter, whose simplicity of execution is made surpassingly clear. Velázquez had been accustomed to painting the heir to the throne ever since the prince's earliest years (one of these childhood portraits is in the Boston museum). The lively trot of the horse seen from below, together with the beauty and finesse of the colors, and the superlative head of the boy prince, laid in with a light coat of paint that lends itself to masterly abbreviations and to smooth, shadowless modelling, all this constitutes a decisive landmark in the painter's work. And in these portraits of the child and his father, the landscapist in Velázquez has made marked progress in the representation of nature. What we have

Prince Don Baltasar Carlos as a Huntsman, 1635-1636. Prado, Madrid.

Prince Don Baltasar Carlos as a Huntsman (detail), 1635-1636. Prado, Madrid.

here are no longer, as has sometimes been said, mere backdrops. We stand before carefully studied transcriptions of the panorama of Sierras and oak forests which surround Madrid, and in which, as Paul Claudel was to put it, "the mountains dance in a ring in chorus." The view corresponds to Velázquez' favorite lookout: the snowy peak in the distance, to the right of the prince's horse, is the Montaña de la Maliciosa in the central chain of the Sierra de Guadarrama.

The series of hunting portraits offers a new combination of the human figure and landscape. They were finished toward 1636, but the Infante Don Fernando, who is portrayed in one of them, had been absent from Madrid since 1632. So Velázquez must have painted his portrait from an earlier head study. The portrait of Prince Baltasar is a charming work. The posing, the naturalness and simplicity of these hunting portraits represent a step forward in the career of Velázquez and in his vocation as a landscape painter, for here he shows an amazing boldness of execution and a great freedom of touch. Velázquez has fully accepted animals, God's creatures, into his world. Seldom does an animal painter succeed in penetrating so deeply into the life-sources of noble animals.

Not many years were left to the Count-Duke to wield his power when Velázquez painted a portrait of him on horseback, probably in 1638. This, as Beruete said, is the very apotheosis of pride, that pride which grows inordinately in great ones as they approach their downfall. That of Olivares was now at hand. The Buen Retiro, whose decorations and entertainments were to remain as the symbol of a frivolous reign, had been his creation. In the ashes of remembrance, now that the palace has been destroyed and its masters have vanished from the earth, all that lives on for us are the music of Calderón's verses and a few paintings by Velázquez.

The Court Dwarf Don Sebastián de Morra, 1644. Prado, Madrid.

THE GRANDEUR AND MISERY OF MAN

"A good portrait always appears to me
like a dramatized biography, or rather like the
natural drama inherent in every man."
BAUDELAIRE, *1859 Salon*.

I N the decade beginning in 1640, the life of Velázquez, hitherto uneventful, entered on a more agitated phase. Events followed hard upon one another: the fall of Olivares, frequent journeys to accompany the king, the death of the young Prince Don Baltasar Carlos, heir to the throne, war and unrest in the kingdom, and finally a second journey to Italy.

There can be no question here of discussing all the paintings of Velázquez, but in order to understand the rich and complex texture of his production, it should be borne in mind that several parallel series of pictures developed at the same pace within the body of his work. Their chronology, never absolutely certain, and the advantage of considering these groups in their entirety allow us to single out at least the following series: religious paintings (*St Anthony Abbot and St Paul the Hermit* and the *Coronation of the Virgin*); mythological subjects, beginning with *Vulcan's Forge*; and portraits of court jesters.

Velázquez liked to seek relaxation from his official duties in painting the picaresque figures around him, dwarfs, court fools, and other hangers-on in the palace. This was not the first time in history that a king took pleasure in surrounding himself with such strange and miserable creatures; but the Baroque court of Philip IV teemed with them. They came under all sorts of headings: professional jesters, dwarfs, harmless fools, freaks and degenerates. How else is this cortege of misery around the great of the earth to be accounted for, if not by the strange attraction exerted by the abnormal individuality making spectacularly evident the enigma of the *principium individuationis*? Velázquez could not fail to take an interest in this phenomenon, possessed as he was, ever since his youth, by what I have called the aesthetic of the individual's salvation.

The Court Jester Calabacillas ("The Idiot of Coria"), c. 1639.
Prado, Madrid.

The bulk of these pictures of buffoons, with the exception perhaps of *The Geographer*, seem to have been painted after his return from Italy in 1631; entries in the palace archives, brought to light some years ago by Moreno Villa, bear this out. The full-length portrait of "Pablillos de Valladolid," of about 1632, is the first representation of a figure surrounded by space without any reference to perspective. Manet had it in mind when he painted *The Fifer*. "Don Juan of Austria," a wily buffoon who had derisively assumed the name of Philip II's glorious son, was painted about 1633, and "Barbarossa," a mad-cap swashbuckler,

The Court Dwarf Francisco Lezcano ("The Child of Vallecas"), 1644. Prado, Madrid.

The Court Dwarf Don Diego de Acedo ("El Primo"), 1644. Prado, Madrid.

shortly after that date. The two pictures entitled *Aesopus* and *Menippus* represent not actual court jesters, but two would-be philosophers. In the latter the dark tones appear to symbolize the servitudes of poverty, accepted however with an undaunted smile. The still life, which in the early works of Seville had such full-bodied volumes, is now reduced to shadowed planes which little by little lose their consistency and substance. In this delineation of the grandeur and misery of man, the four portraits painted by Velázquez of the court dwarfs represent the climax of a passionate investigation. A categorical warning against taking any pride in the human condition, this teratological repertory might be styled the "polyptych of freaks." The picture of the jester Calabacillas, sometimes mistakenly called the "idiot of Coria," no doubt begun before 1639, was later retouched; the three other dwarfs, El Primo, Don Sebastián de Morra, and Francisco Lezcano, the so-called "child of Vallecas," must have been painted at Saragossa in 1644. Working unhurriedly from these patient models, Velázquez abstracted himself from the harassing preoccupations that darkened the journey of the court.

These were bitter years for Spain: Portugal rebelled, the French invaded Catalonia, Olivares was dismissed, Sicily and Naples rose in arms, the nobles of Aragon and Andalusia conspired against the king, and the queen died, followed—fatal misfortune—by Baltasar Carlos, heir to the throne. Shortly before the prince's death, Velázquez had painted him in the picture in the Vienna museum, which is like the quintessence of the court portrait as he conceived it to be. The figure is seen full length, three-quarter face, or roughly so. The right arm is extended in a gesture expressing will and power, while the graceful curve of the left arm compensates for this authoritarian stiffness. The legs are firmly planted on the ground. Generally a red and gold upholstered armchair and a table spread with velvet make up a summary *mise en scène*. The background is divided into dark and light rectangles. Velázquez kept to a formula that had held good since the sixteenth century, and he was obliged to modifiy it scarcely at all in order to give

Prince Don Baltasar Carlos, c. 1640. Kunsthistorisches Museum, Vienna.

King Philip IV at Fraga, 1644. Frick Collection, New York.

it an archetypal value and to deepen the picture space. The portrait takes on an ambivalent, almost contradictory aspect: at once calm and dynamic in a composition of absolute clarity. The model's restful pose is charged with potential action. "Without any of the violence of a Tintoretto or a Daumier," writes Mayer, "these figures act like forces in space... Velázquez plumbs space in all direction."

When we extol the astonishing lifelikeness of these portraits by Velázquez, or the freedom of his technique made up of "distant spots" (as Quevedo described it) which anticipate Impressionism, it is well to remember that the first virtue of the painter lies in his total, unitary conception of the picture, in his construction in terms of forms. It is here that the artist shows his creative genius, and Velázquez does not fail to show his, although he does so with a discretion not always to be found in modern painters. Simplicity, measure, love of essentials, guide his brush. Mayer put it perfectly when he wrote, "What we admire above all in Velázquez is the instinctive sureness of his self-mastery. Everything in him is necessary: nothing is excessive, nothing is insufficient. From this results harmony in the attitude, in the composition, in the color scheme, in the expression." At a far remove from the view of Velázquez taken by the narrow-minded realists of the nineteenth century, Mayer draws all the inferences from this new comprehension: "The painting of Velázquez corresponds to the final form of the Greek vision of the natural, not in any outwardly naturalistic imitation, but in a simplifying realism which always ennobles nature, fortifies human qualities, and does away with the vulgarity of everything it touches. Without imitating the ancients, and even though setting himself in deliberate opposition to everything that goes by the name of the classical tradition, Velázquez, like Raphael before him, endows his creations with a clarity and self-evidence which in the end amounts to a kind of classicism." The Raphael of the Baroque age, such was Velázquez as seen by Mayer, and Beruete wrote that he was "more than a naturalist, because he did not content himself with reproducing a perishable form, but endeavored to penetrate its essence." Compare his portraits with those by other

Pope Innocent X, 1650. Galleria Doria Pamphili, Rome.

painters—Rubens, Van Dyck—of the same models: Philip IV, Isabelle de Bourbon, Don Fernando, Spinola. What for Velázquez is the essential dissolves in the others into mere lifelikeness and decorative adjuncts.

Velázquez was never so great a colorist as in the portrait of Philip IV in military costume (Frick Collection, New York) and in that of Pope Innocent X (Galleria Doria Pamphili, Rome). The first was made in three sittings which the king granted his painter in the town of Fraga, in Aragon. The work was done in a makeshift studio fitted up on the spur of the moment, in a small room with shattered walls and no flooring, during a brief halt in the field in the course of the campaign of 1644. In this bare room Velázquez worked as if he had been in a palace. This is perhaps the richest, most perfect portrait he ever made of his master. This harmony of pinks, blacks and silvery tints is one of the world's most exquisite, most sumptuous pieces of painting. His versatility enabled Velázquez to pass without any transition from this delightful work to the portraits of dwarfs, of which he seems to have painted at least three that same year, in the course of the same journey into Aragon. Under his profoundly human brush, these monsters inspire no feelings of repulsion. These pictures may be regarded as marking the climax of his passion for representing the individual. His love of life, which made him faithful to the mute exactitude of appearances, led him to plumb these unhappy creatures and to bring out, in their expression and gaze, the sediment common to us all, which gives to each existence a sufficient dignity. Incapable of lying, either before a king or before a buffoon, possessed by a need of transcendent truthfulness, he seems each time to be trying to understand his models with the best intentions of God.

This is the very attitude, ethically and aesthetically unexceptionable, which Velázquez adopted toward the highest ranking personage who ever sat to him, Pope Innocent X. This unforgettable portrait is a monument of Western history. The pope cannot be said by any means to have an attractive face. This old Roman aristocrat of seventy-five, narrow-minded, with his grim, mistrustful glance, his thinning hair, his puffed and blotchy cheeks, was the least desirable of models for a painter

*View of the Gardens of the
Villa Medici in Rome (Midday),
1650-1651. Prado, Madrid.*

of princes and grandees. Faithful to his implacable objectivity, the
Spaniard made no effort to flatter so thankless a sitter, yet what dignity,
what grandeur he gave him! Schopenhauer said that in front of this
picture one has the impression of standing before a majesty of the earth.
This impression springs from a purely aesthetic quality: the monumentality which Velázquez succeeded in imparting to the form, and which
lies not in its size but in the expressive arrangement of lines and of the
composition. So effective are the beautifully contrived accord of reds,
whites and golds, and the abbreviated, synthetic execution of color
patches, laid on in bold strokes, that this arresting portrait takes us by

*View of the Gardens of the
Villa Medici in Rome (Afternoon),
1650-1651. Prado, Madrid.*

surprise even when we come to analyze its details. Looking at this painting, as at those of princes and court jesters, we can say again with Carl Justi that Velázquez has painted "the tone of the nerves, the quality of the vital sap, the proportion of iron and bile in the blood, of prudence and folly in the brain." Nowhere else do we better feel the truth of another of Justi's observations: "Compared with that of Velázquez, Titian's coloring seems conventional, Rembrandt's fantastic, and Rubens's affected with mannerism." For Sir Joshua Reynolds the portrait of Innocent X was the "best painting in Rome," and this was the supreme compliment in the mouth of the great English portraitist.

*The Lady with a Fan
(Portrait of the Artist's Daughter
Francisca), c. 1646.
Wallace Collection, London.*

Rome also offered Velázquez an opportunity of giving us an
intimate testimony of his lyrical feeling for landscape: the two small
pictures showing views of the gardens of the Villa Medici. In one the
light of midday, in the other that of the afternoon, in both a synthetic,
allusive execution and an exquisite sense of poetry, bring to mind, two
centuries in advance, the subtlest, most delicate notations of Corot.

At this same period, Velázquez, whose rare production always offers
facets of rich variety, also painted some masterly portraits of children
(the one owned by the Hispanic Society of America, in New York, may
be the artist's grand-daughter) and of women. The *Lady with a Fan*

(Wallace Collection, London) is the most remarkable representation we have of the Spanish woman in her gracious reserve. It is very possible that this is Velázquez' daughter Francisca. A portrait of Archbishop Valdés is now in the National Gallery, London, and Velázquez is known to have painted a portrait of Cardinal Borgia which has been lost, but of which some replicas remain, and above all an impressive chalk drawing (Academy of San Fernando, Madrid), one of the few sure and perfect examples of Velázquez' work as a draftsman.

To paint the grave and noble figure of a woman in the *Coronation of the Virgin* in the Prado, he had no need to depart very much from everyday humanity. In the same way, the two views of the Villa Medici simply voice, more intimately and personally, the serene and tender feeling for landscape which we find again in the picture of *St Anthony Abbot and St Paul the Hermit*, also in the Prado. Lastly, in the same vein of inspiration, there are the vast landscapes with hunting scenes, views of architecture, foliage in the gardens of Aranjuez, of which at least the delightful little figures owe something to the master's touch. This is a much disputed group of works, in which the participation of Mazo is generally recognized. It is impossible, however, to banish the idea that there is something of Velázquez' brush in these charming and masterly works.

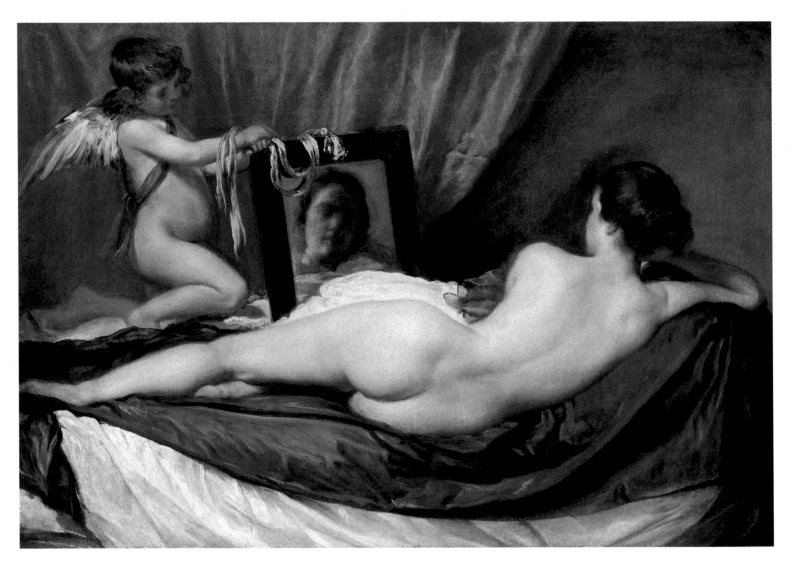

Venus and Cupid ("The Rokeby Venus"), c. 1648-1650.
National Gallery, London.

THE PARADOX OF REALITY

"Just as Descartes reduces thought to rationality, so Velázquez reduces painting to visuality."

JOSÉ ORTEGA Y GASSET.

P RESENT reality taken as the mainstay of the art of painting, this was the essential inspiration of Velázquez. But this inevitable presence, the prose and prop of our lives, has not, as might be imagined, merely a single significance. The plastic reality that Velázquez offers us in his early works is founded on what Berenson calls *tactile values*; in other words, on a semblance, intended to deceive the eye, of what we perceive through the sense of touch, of hardness, consistency, volumes, profiles. Starting out from this point, Velázquez proceeded to transform his painting by bending it to the evolution of his vision, which was ably served by an increasingly perfected technique. In time, more and more effectively, this initial reality was purged, synthesized, and finally overcome by the painter. Pure vision is the image, in an inaccessible space, that a mirror gives us. In a mirror, vision takes on the character of a concept: things are or are not, exist or vanish, just as to Calderón life appeared to be a dream, and dream life. Mirrors, as Pedro Penzol has pointed out, play an important role in several paintings by Velázquez. He was fond of them; in the inventory of his household belongings drawn up after his death, ten mirrors are listed. There comes to mind at once the picture in which a lovely Spanish woman, with slender waist and full hips, turns her back on us, out of disdain or coquetry. She chooses not to show her face, but equivocally reveals it to us in her looking glass, dim and ghostly. This is the Rokeby *Venus*. It is safe to say that this was neither the only Venus nor the only female nude Velázquez painted; but none other has come down to us. The prevailing opinion today is that the picture in the National Gallery of London was painted before 1651. A matchless color harmony tempers the warm Venetian tonality and Rubensian opulence with a graver, more Spanish accord of whites, leaden grays, blue and carmines, to which is added the brown ivory of the flesh tint. But most important of all here is the fact that the painter holds more aloof from appearances; his immediate perception of the tangible grows blurred; contours melt away and reality becomes more and more remote and paradoxical.

The mythological paintings in which, ever since his *Vulcan* and his *Mars*, Velázquez had been seeking atmospheric effects also lent themselves to this equivocal play, no doubt unconscious on the artist's part, and rather the fruit of intuition than of reasoning. Of the pictures on pagan themes which Velázquez painted for the Salón de los Espejos in the royal palace—mirrors again—in the last decade of his life, three perished in the terrible fire that ravaged the Alcázar in 1734; had it not been for this disaster, the Prado today would be richer to an even more fabulous degree than it is. All that now remains is the *Mercury and Argus*, painted about 1659, and it is a fine example of that almost bodiless painting to which the art of Velázquez attained in the end. This manner of painting, supremely light in texture, with a vagueness of outline which reduces bodies to an almost ghostly state, already appears in the "polyptych of freaks" and in the portrait of Pope Innocent X.

The main task that fell to Velázquez upon his return from Italy in 1651 was not too well suited to his bent toward this immaterial kind of painting, but he brought to bear on it the extreme subtlety of his technique. He had to paint portraits, a great many portraits, intended for very specific purposes: to immortalize, with force and distinction, first the king's new bride, the young Mariana of Austria, his niece, then the Infanta María Teresa, in whom the Habsburg features were enhanced by those of her mother, Isabelle de Bourbon. Soon came the children of Philip IV and Queen Mariana, the Infanta Margarita and the Infante Felipe Prosper, heir to the throne, who died however before he reached the age of three. The intensity of his colors is greater than ever, and his palette brighter. Carmines, silvery tints and vermilions form, as it were, a crescendo in the great fugue of Velázquez' final style. It is as if the painter, having deepened his insight into his models, were drawing from

The Infanta María Teresa, c. 1652. Kunsthistorisches Museum, Vienna.

them a more intense and at the same time more intimate note, especially in the portraits of children, who always so much appealed to him and quickened his inspiration. His technique, more and more abbreviated as time went on, reduced tactile values to chromatic allusions.

A study of these portraits shows the rich gamut of harmonies then dominant in the painter's palette. Mariana of Austria, like a royal doll, rouged and powdered, has a majestic and solemn air in spite of her monstrous gown, whose black velvet sets off the silver trimmings. Against this sober color scheme rings out the rich note struck by carmines, vermilions and golds. A haughty idol, such is the new queen,

The Infanta Margarita, c. 1656.
Kunsthistorisches Museum, Vienna.

The Infanta Margarita in Blue, c. 1659.
Kunsthistorisches Museum, Vienna.

niece and wife of Philip IV, who had once entertained hopes of marrying her to his son, the ill-starred prince Baltasar Carlos.

Like Goya, Velázquez had the knack of adapting himself to his models and swathing them in an orchestration of colors inspired by their character and physiognomy. Making no display of psychology, he instinctively chose from his palette the harmony of tones best suited to the person portrayed, brought out with convincing elegance his or her personality, and surrounded it with a well-defined spiritual atmosphere whose undertones he varied according to the model's character.

The Infanta Margarita, c. 1660. Kunsthistorisches Museum, Vienna.

The series of family portraits sent to the court at Vienna, and unusually well preserved in the great museum of the old Imperial city, offers a perfect example of this skill and exquisite taste. In order to grasp clearly the two poles of the art of Velázquez, whose aesthetic embraced human grandeur as well as human misery, we can do no better than compare what we have called the "polyptych of freaks" with a parallel series of paintings, that polyptych of beauty and grace on the walls of the Vienna museum. It was the good fortune of the Imperial court to receive, in pictures by Velázquez, the most delightful embassy possible. The Infanta María Teresa, daughter of Isabelle de Bourbon, was the loveliest feminine ornament of the court of Madrid, and her future marriage was one of the cornerstones of Spanish foreign policy; with the Rokeby *Venus* and the *Lady with a Fan*, she deserves to figure in any anthology of the most beautiful women painted by Velázquez. To bring out her distinction and youth with sobriety, he chose silvery accents —her jewels and handkerchief—and lines lightly underscored with rosy carmine—her neck, arms and headdress. And to make the bright and luminous richness of her person stand out better, he surrounded it with velvety green.

It is this unostentatious distinction that makes Velázquez' paintings appear of so manifest an excellence and simplicity, a simplicity that seems to raise no problems. His style resides precisely in this sobriety, which may be called classical. But when we approach the picture for a look at the details, everything vibrates, grows indistinct, and scintillates in the isolated dabs of each brushstroke. The painter's analysis of his model consists in breaking it down into purposeful color patches charged with a synthetic power which already allows for the fusion of these separate touches when seen at a distance. The spirited lightness of his brush is best exemplified in jewels, plumes and hair which, when seen at close range, appear to be so many shapeless dabs of paint. The enchantment of childhood is conveyed in the supreme refinement of colors which seem predestined to express tenderness. Such is the portrait of the Infanta Margarita with a vase of flowers, of about 1653, also in

The Infanta María Teresa (detail), c. 1652. Kunsthistorisches Museum, Vienna.

The Infanta Margarita in Blue (detail), c. 1659.
Kunsthistorisches Museum, Vienna.

Vienna. The rose that has fallen from the vase is, in its pictorial execution, a piece of pure abstraction such as a present-day painter might have produced. A silvery gray sings out alongside golds and reds in the later portrait of the Infanta Margarita, made about 1656, which served as a study for *Las Meninas*. The position of the arms accentuates the triangular composition of the silhouette founded on the hoop skirt,

Prince Felipe Prosper, 1659. Kunsthistorisches Museum, Vienna.

whose awkward, bulky framework thus fits smoothly into the picture pattern and color scheme invented by the painter.

Some three years later, in 1659, again for the court of Vienna, he painted the portrait of the short-lived heir to the Spanish throne, born of the king's second marriage, Prince Felipe Prosper. In this, perhaps the finest portrait of a child in all European painting, Velázquez, as in his portrait of Innocent X, sought to pay to his future Catholic Majesty —doomed in this case to an early death—the sumptuous homage of color. The problems of space receding in depth and the rich furnishings of chairs, curtains and rugs contribute to present the figure of the royal child with supreme, almost miraculous simplicity; and answering to the child, in a kind of sprightly counterpoint, is the little white dog silhouetted against the deep red velvet of the miniature armchair. The lightness of the texture, the scumbles as subtle as in a watercolor, the color scheme of silver gray and pink, are all remarkable. And Velázquez painted the dog with no less loving care than the child. His human sympathy went in equal measure to all God's creatures.

In this same year, 1659, he was again called on to paint the Infanta Margarita who, though only eight years old, became a candidate for an imperial betrothal, now that the marriage of her sister María Teresa with Louis XIV of France had been decided on. Though still so young, she had to be represented—and this was the purpose of the portrait—with a royal dignity symbolizing her future destiny. A blue farthingale trimmed with gold and silver, the rich texture of her fur muff, and the dark, noble reflections of furniture in the background give this work a severer harmony than in the previous portraits of the Infanta. The child appears about to hold an audience. There is perhaps an even greater boldness in the execution and details, and passages might be singled out so rich and full-bodied in color, so free in form and handling, that they surpass the most inspired painting of the best abstract *tachiste* of our century. The exquisite lavishness of the texture, the nervous, life-enhancing vibrancy, and the incredible lightness of touch make these fragments so many anthology pieces heralding the finest

Half-Length Portrait of King Philip IV, c. 1655. Prado, Madrid.

discoveries of the modern sensibility and confirming the truth of Justi's comment: "It is as if he set out to demonstrate that poetry can be extracted from prose and... the fanciful from the natural." Remember too the question which, well in advance of his time, the great German critic asked himself in front of other pictures by the Spanish master: "Could it be that in art the object is nothing and the language everything?" This question points the way to the modern aesthetic. It raises the problem of the liberties taken by the painter in his interpretation. And with this consideration El Greco, Velázquez, Goya, and the boldest of contemporary painters are seen to fall in line with each other.

The "brutal sketches" for which Pacheco had condemned El Greco appeared now in the work of Velázquez, but with him they served another purpose. It is only by isolating and enlarging particular details, which photography today makes easy, that we can be brought to realize how very far Velázquez was carried by his revolutionary attitude. His great simplicity and his sober, refined taste in the presentation of the figure now bore their final fruit, for example in the half-length portrait of Philip IV in the Prado. This intimate effigy of the king, a sadder and wiser man, awaking to the consciousness of his wasted life, is indeed the last picture that the visitor to the Prado should see, in his pilgrimage to the sanctuary of Velázquez' art. Lefort has described the impression it made on him: "This painting makes all its formidable neighbors seem to us like set images; lifeless or conventional: Van Dyck heavy, Rubens stodgy, and Tintoretto sallow. Velázquez alone gives us, in all its plenitude, the illusion of life." Yes, and how far he is already from Caravaggio and Caravaggism! Consider the head of this king and you will agree with Ruskin, even though his choice of names may seem to you too arbitrary or personal, that if we merely want to count the hairs on a head, a poster painter or an anatomist will do very well, but to represent the few that are visible is a matter only for the supreme masters, Carpaccio, Tintoretto, Reynolds or Velázquez.

We now know that the famous picture always called *Las Hilanderas* (the *Spinners* or *Tapestry Weavers*) actually represents a mythological theme: Pallas and Arachne. True to his methods, he reduces the fantastic to an allusion, he withdraws and attenuates the anecdote. The story unfolds only on the tapestry hanging in the background. As in his early work, *Christ in the House of Martha and Mary*, everyday reality occupies the foreground, here in the guise of a tapestry workshop. The true subject is the light that plays over bodies and makes them unreal, haloing the background figures with its strongest beams or reducing them to a curtain of indistinct forms melting into the penumbra. By setting the subject in a tapestry workshop, Velázquez found for it the logarithm of reality defined by Ortega, and Américo Castro considers that the mythological theme is no more important in the picture than the fact of having embodied the abstract figures of the fable in Spanish women spinning and threading yarn and in aristocratic ladies looking at the tapestry. But, most important of all, these figures are reduced pictorially to pure color values, to forms dissolved in light, to "distant patches," to a transfigured reality. The great writer Quevedo, a contemporary of the artist, dedicated these lines to him, in which, in his Baroque style, he expressed already these very ideas:

"From the light support of the painting,
the color flees like shadow,
denying the relief the hand would find."

The picture of the *Tapestry Weavers* shows us how Velázquez' method and his vision of nature have accentuated his highly personal procedure of eliminating plastic modelling, or rather of reducing it to pure color values, to almost flat forms floating in light and space. The painting thus becomes pure appearance, pure visuality, reality subjectivated to the extreme limit, to the point where it seems about to vanish. This is the paradox of reality admitted only in so far as it constitutes a presence for us. Searching out the basis of truth, which would enable him to construct the world intellectually, Descartes arrived at the formula "I think, therefore I am." The sole basis of existence is in the thought, the awareness, that each man has of himself. Pursuing the parallel so acutely emphasized by Ortega y Gasset, I might

The Tapestry Weavers or The Fable of Arachne ("Las Hilanderas"),
1657-1660. Prado, Madrid.

say that for Velázquez, from the painter's visual point of view, real
existence has as its sole basis the pure appearance that one finds in oneself
and the pure color values in which lines, volumes, bodies, and tactile
values are diluted. The thing pictured becomes the ghost of itself. The
purpose of the *Tapestry Weavers*, as of the *Maids of Honor*, is to give a
definitive formulation of this pictorial testament of Velázquez.

The Maids of Honor ("Las Meninas"), 1656. Prado, Madrid.

If we can speak of impressionism in connection with Velázquez, this, as Oskar Hagen has noted, is because he succeeded in representing things just as they appear, as a shapeless aggregate of colored planes. The volumes of his early paintings, with their hard, polished contours, have become apparitions no less ghostly for being real or present to us. In the *Maids of Honor*, the Baroque painting *par excellence*, where is the picture, where is the reality? We are told that the artist has portrayed himself in the act of painting the royal couple, dimly visible in a mirror at the back of the room. But what is offered us is the group of bystanders watching the royal couple pose: the little Infanta, her maids of honor and retinue gathered around her. The subject of the picture is not on the canvas but in the space where the beholder stands. The figures themselves are looking at what is presumably the subject, whose place we ourselves occupy as we look at them. Under the play of lights and shadows, forms melt away. The focal unity of the picture is centered on the blond hair of the Infanta; from this point, everything runs off like the notes of a fugue and loses every value save its pure relation to the other notes. The brooch on the Infanta's breast, her little hand resting on her hoop skirt, the bright gleams in the women's hair and on the silk of their gowns, the large head and coarse features of the dwarf, the spectral shadows of the steward and the duenna—in all this there is nothing now but vague forms in process of dissolution. But then, to bring us back to reality, there is the artist himself who seems to be painting us; and to prove to us that light alone gives existence to form, there, at the farthest point from the eye, is the open door, with sunlight pouring in from behind and the courtier pausing on the steps, who serves as a screen and gives an idea of the distances in the room. Pure visuality, pure appearance—this paradoxical reality defies commentary. And this is why the ultimate secret of a great work of art remains forever impenetrable.

Classical or Renaissance art constructs its ideal types and fixes its canons of beauty by abstracting certain elements from reality: line, form, design, mathematical or rational space, and what Leonardo called "universal light." The nominalist art of Velázquez falls back on the

The Maids of Honor ("Las Meninas"), detail: Self-Portrait, 1656. Prado, Madrid.

The Maids of Honor ("Las Meninas"), detail: The Infanta Margarita, 1656. Prado, Madrid.

world of man, on the everyday world, on visual appearances, thanks to which things overflow their outlines and reduce the entity of volumes to pure color patches, and space to atmospheric values. But with the visual sincerity of his subjective picture order, Velázquez perceives and reflects the instantaneity of a single moment, which can never repeat itself. He sought to record time in the spatial vision that painting offers us, thereby enabling us to salvage something of passing time. The classical masters aspired to perpetuate ideas, symbols of perfect but timeless beauties. Velázquez aspired to immortalize man in the flesh, and to capture the poetry of the fleeting instant. This lyrical, suggestive manner of responding to the mystery of existence is what makes him the first modern painter.

Prince Felipe Prosper (detail), 1659.
Kunsthistorisches Museum, Vienna.

BIOGRAPHY AND BACKGROUND

LIST OF ILLUSTRATIONS

BIOGRAPHY AND BACKGROUND

1597 **Marriage in Seville on December 28 of the painter's parents, Juan Rodríguez de Silva and Jerónima Velázquez, both born in Seville, but of Portuguese stock, the family of both coming originally from Porto. In signing his pictures, the painter always used his mother's surname.**

1598 Death of King Philip II, succeeded by Philip III, king of Spain, Sicily, Naples and Portugal.
Birth of Francisco Zurbarán in Estremadura.

1599 **Birth in Seville of Diego Rodríguez de Silva y Velázquez, probably on June 5; he was baptized the next day in the church of San Pedro.**

1603 First journey to Spain of Peter Paul Rubens (born 1577). Sent there by Vincenzo Gonzaga, Duke of Mantua, with a variety of presents for Philip III and his minister the Duke of Lerma, Rubens landed at Alicante and went on to Valladolid where the king was sojourning. In Spain he painted several portraits, in particular the *Equestrian Portrait of the Duke of Lerma*.

1609 **Velázquez enters the studio of the painter Francisco Herrera the Elder, one of the initiators of the new naturalistic trend of Sevillian painting in the early seventeenth century. He stays only a few months.**

1609-1611 Expulsion of the Moriscos (Spanish Moors). The number driven out is estimated at 275,000. A measure of great cruelty, and harmful to the Spanish economy.

1610 **Apprenticed to Francisco Pacheco, an academic painter and art historian whose Seville studio was a busy center of the local art life. A fellow apprentice is Alonso Cano, sculptor, painter and architect, later one of the masters of Spanish Baroque.**

1611 **Francisco Pacheco and Velázquez' father sign a contract, whereby Pacheco engages to teach the boy "the art of painting" for a period of six years.**

1614 Death of El Greco in Toledo, where he had lived and worked since 1577.
Zurbarán is sent by his father to Seville and there enters the studio of Juan de las Roelas.

1616 Pacheco appointed censor of works of art by the grand inquisitor of Seville.

1617 **Velázquez' bond of apprenticeship ends and he qualifies as a master, entering the Seville painters' guild and thus obtaining the right to exercise his art in all parts of the kingdom.**

1617 Birth of Murillo in Seville.
Zurbarán leaves Seville for Llerna.

1618 Marriage on April 23, in Seville, of Diego Velázquez and Juana de Miranda Pacheco, daughter of his master.

1619 Baptism on May 18 of Francisca, the artist's first daughter.

1620 Diego de Melgar bound as apprentice to Velázquez for a period of six years.

1621 Baptism on January 29 of Ignacia, the artist's second daughter, who dies in infancy.

> 1621 Death of Philip III, succeeded by Philip IV. The new king's favorite was Don Gaspar de Guzmán, Count-Duke of Olivares, who acted as chief minister until 1643.

1622 Accompanied by Melgar, Velázquez pays a short visit to Madrid in the spring, visiting the Escorial and painting a portrait of Góngora.

1623 Invited back to Madrid by Olivares himself, he returns to the capital in the summer with his father-in-law Pacheco and his pupil and servant Juan de Pareja. He receives fifty ducats for moving expenses and on October 6 he is appointed painter to the king with a monthly salary of twenty ducats. Settles now in Madrid with his family.

1624 Commissioned to paint portraits of King Philip IV, Olivares and several prominent courtiers.

1625 Exhibits in the Calle Mayor an equestrian portrait of Philip IV. Much admired, it is vaunted in a sonnet by Pacheco.

1627 Competition sponsored by the king among his four court painters on the theme of the Expulsion of the Moriscos. Velázquez wins and on March 7 is appointed Gentleman Usher.
Portraits by Velázquez (now lost) of Philip IV and Olivares are sent to the Duke of Mantua by his envoy in Spain, who speaks of the artist as "the most famous painter in this country."

1628 On September 3 the king orders the Armería to provide Velázquez with anything he may need to paint the portrait of the late King Philip III and grants him a daily ration of food supplies equal to that received by the court barbers.

> 1628 Rubens in Madrid again on a diplomatic mission, for nine months, and the king appoints Velázquez to be his guide among the art treasures of Spain. The two men become close friends.
> Zurbarán appointed official painter to the city of Seville, where he lives and works for the next thirty years.

1629 Velázquez obtains leave from the king to visit Italy. Sailing from Barcelona he reaches Genoa on August 20. Whether or not he had any secret mission, his own purpose, as he told the ambassador of Parma in Spain, was to "improve himself in his profession." From Genoa he goes to Milan, then to Venice. In October, travelling via Ferrara, Cento, Bologna and Loreto, he arrives in Rome, where he spends a year.

1630 He pays a visit to Naples, where he meets the Spanish painter Jusepe de Ribera, master of the dramatic chiaroscuro known as Tenebrismo, who had settled there in 1616. Velázquez returns to Madrid in January 1631.

1634 Marriage of his daughter Francisca with the painter Juan Bautista Martínez del Mazo, his pupil and assistant, who now succeeds him as Gentleman Usher, Velázquez himself receiving steady promotion in the royal household.

1634-1636 Zurbarán in Madrid, doing decorative paintings for Philip IV in the Buen Retiro Palace.

1637 Alonso Cano settles in Madrid at the invitation of Olivares.

1638 Visit to Madrid in the autumn of Francesco I d'Este, Duke of Modena, and Velázquez begins his portrait. He presents the duke with a small portrait of the king (lost) "so lifelike and so fine that one fairly marvels at it."

1639 The Este ambassador in Madrid writes to Duke Francesco at Modena: "His work is dear, but how well he works, for I hold his portraits to be nowise inferior to those of the most celebrated artists both ancient and modern."

1640 Death of Rubens in Antwerp.

1642 In the spring he accompanies the king into Aragon, where they spend several months. He obtains permission for Murillo to copy paintings in the royal palaces.

1643 Appointed Superintendent of the Royal Collections with a further salary of sixty ducats a month.

1643 French victory over the Spanish at Rocroi, leading to Olivares' fall from power.

1644 Death of the king's wife, Isabella of Bourbon.
Death of Pope Urban VIII, succeeded by Innocent X.

1646 Appointed Gentleman of the Bedchamber, he is called upon to play an important part in the official ceremonies.

1646 Death of Philip IV's sister Doña María and of Prince Don Baltasar Carlos, his eldest son and heir.

1648 Velázquez' yearly pension, for portraits painted and to be painted, is increased to 700 ducats. He leaves Madrid with the Spanish delegation bound for Trent to fetch the king's new bride, Archduchess Mariana of Austria.

1648 Visit to Madrid of the Dutch painter Gerard Terborch.

1649 Sails on January 21 from Málaga with the Spanish delegation to Italy, landing at Genoa. Travels overland to Venice, where he is the guest of the Spanish ambassador, the Marquis de la Fuente: there, for the royal collections, he buys Titians, Tintorettos and Veroneses. After seeing the Correggios in Bologna, he journeys on to Modena, Parma and Florence, then to Rome and on to Naples, where he spends a month, seeing again his old friend Ribera. By July 10 he is back in Rome for a long stay.

1649 Publication in Seville of Pacheco's book *El arte de la pintura, su antigüedad y grandeza*, an important source for the history of Spanish painting.

1650 Paints the portrait of Pope Innocent X, described by Sir Joshua Reynolds a hundred years later as "the finest picture in Rome." Elected a member of the Roman Academy of St Luke. Overstays his leave and is pressingly summoned home by the king.

1651 Returns to Madrid via Barcelona in June, a year late, bringing with him many pictures and 300 pieces of statuary, which he afterwards arranged and catalogued for the king.

1652 Appointed by the king to the high post of Marshal of the Royal Household, being sworn in on March 8.

1653 On February 22 the king dispatches to the court of Vienna a portrait of the Infanta María Teresa painted by Velázquez.

1656 Paints "Las Meninas" (The Maids of Honor), his most famous painting, described by Luca Giordano as the "theology of painting" and by Sir Thomas Lawrence as the "philosophy of art." It contains the best portrait we have of the artist, seen standing at his easel.

1657 Applies for permission to return to Italy to seek out a painter capable of doing fresco decorations in the royal palace, but the king refuses to let him go. His son-in-law Mazo is sent instead.

1657-1660 Paints his last great work "Las Hilanderas" (The Tapestry Weavers, or The Fable of Arachne).

1658 Zurbarán settles in Madrid.
1659 Peace of the Pyrenees between France and Spain.

1660 On April 7 Velázquez leaves Madrid for Fuenterrabia in northern Spain, to decorate the royal residence in the Isle of Pheasants for the betrothal of the king's daughter María Teresa with Louis XIV of France. The ceremony takes place on June 7. Returning to Madrid on June 26, he is stricken with fever a few weeks later and dies on August 6. His wife Juana followed him to the grave within a week. Both were interred in the parish church of San Juan Bautista. This church was destroyed by the French in 1811, so that all trace of the tomb is now lost.

LIST OF ILLUSTRATIONS

Unless otherwise specified, all pictures are reproduced from archive photographs.

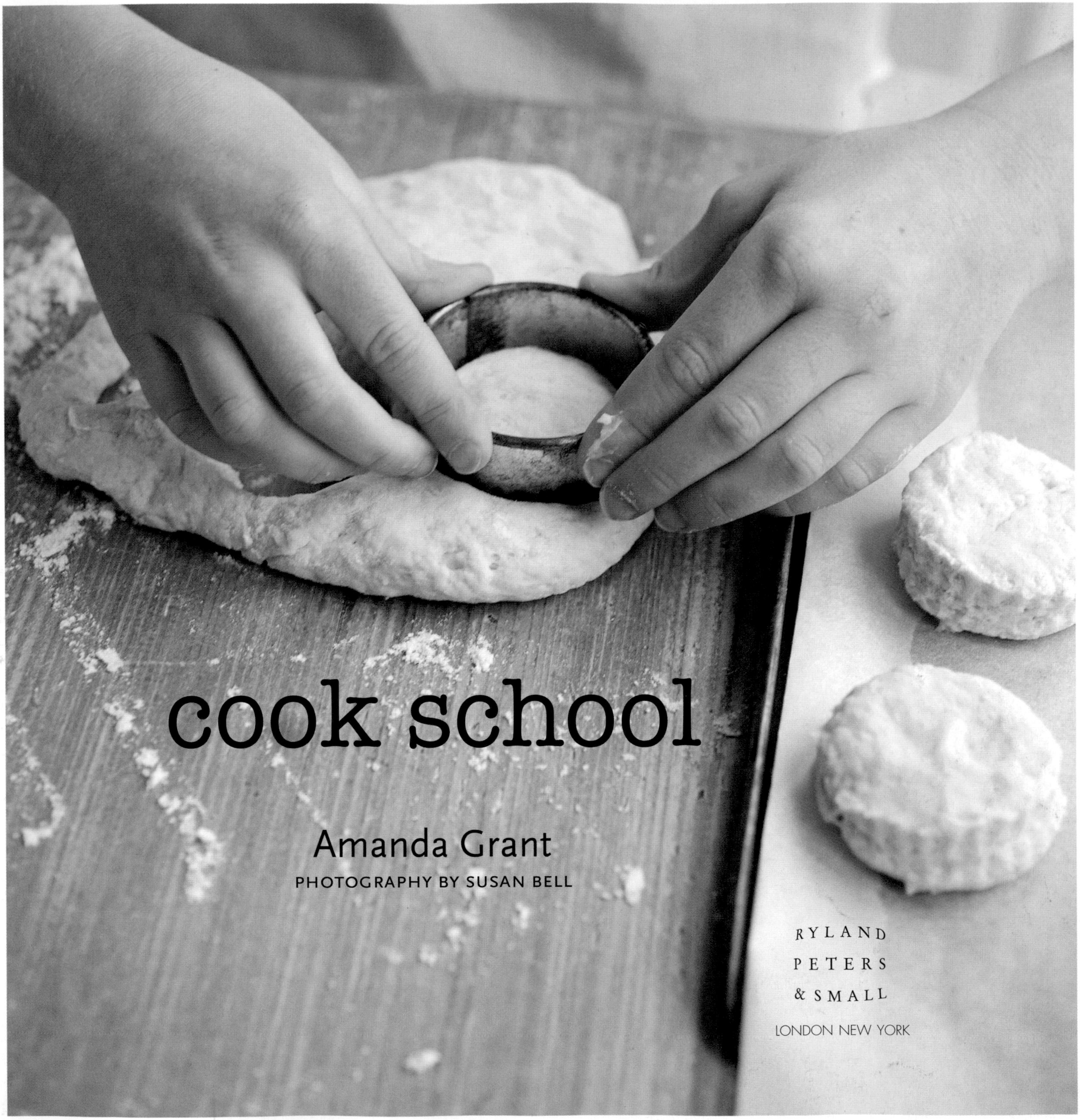

cook school

Amanda Grant

PHOTOGRAPHY BY SUSAN BELL

RYLAND
PETERS
& SMALL

LONDON NEW YORK

For Ethan and Noah, my two new, very special nephews and all the wonderful children who live in our street.

Senior Designer Iona Hoyle
Senior Editor Céline Hughes
Location Researcher Jess Walton
Production Toby Marshall
Publishing Director Alison Starling

Prop and Food Stylist Amanda Grant
Photoshoot Assistants Brenda Bishop and Esther Webb
Indexer Hilary Bird

First published in the US in 2011
by Ryland Peters & Small
519 Broadway, 5th Floor
New York NY 10012
www.rylandpeters.com

10 9 8 7 6 5 4 3 2 1

Text © Amanda Grant 2011
Design and photographs
© Ryland Peters & Small 2011

ISBN: 978-1-84975-136-0

A CIP record for this book is available from the Library of Congress.

Printed in China

NOTES

• All spoon measurements are level unless otherwise specified.
• Ovens should be preheated to the specified temperatures. All ovens work slightly differently. We recommend using an oven thermometer and suggest you consult the maker's handbook for any special instructions, particularly if you are cooking in a fan-assisted oven, as you will need to adjust temperatures according to manufacturer's instructions.
• All eggs are medium, unless otherwise specified. It is recommended that free-range eggs be used.
• Recipes containing raw or partially cooked egg, or raw fish or shellfish, should not be served to the very young, very old, anyone with a compromised immune system or pregnant women.

Neither the author nor the publisher can be held responsible for any claim arising out of the information in this book. Always consult your health advisor or doctor if you have any concerns about your child's health or nutrition.

contents

Foreword by
Marguerite Patten, CBE

Cook School is a practical and inspiring cookery book
for young children.

Amanda Grant has helped parents by producing
excellent books on feeding children. Now she is
showing children how to achieve a sense of
achievement and pleasure by learning to cook.

The accepted method of teaching children to read is
by giving them books, toys and information suitable
for their age. This approach is followed in *Cook School*.

Interesting information and suitable recipes are given
under the ages of 3–5 years, then 5–7 years and 7–11;
in the case of food preparation, physical ability
must also be considered.

Parents will be thrilled by the extra skills their
children will develop.

introduction

THIS BOOK BELONGS TO

....

Put your name in the space above and keep this book somewhere safe. Treasure it and enjoy it! You are about to learn some skills that you can use for the rest of your life. If you start cooking now, you will have lots of fun ahead of you making good food for you and your family and friends.

We all need to eat every day and it is much more exciting if you have helped to make some of those meals, instead of always eating food that others have made for you. Have you ever cooked a meal for anyone? When you do, you will see just how happy it makes people feel and how grateful they are for the time and care you have taken. This will make you feel proud too. It feels good when you cook for others.

THE SKILLS
Learning to cook is a bit like learning to read. When you learn to read, you learn the letters first and then you start to put the letters together to form words. It is similar to this when you learn to cook. You first learn some basic skills that you can later put together to make meals.

Cooking is not just about making something to eat; you will be practicing maths (measuring, weighing, sharing); literacy (reading and writing if you jot down some notes about the recipes), and geography (learning about food and where it comes from) and much more.

Cooking uses all your senses. You can look at food, smell it, touch it, taste it, and listen to it as it cooks. This is something my mom taught me when I was young. I think that's pretty exciting; I hope you do, too.

THE RECIPES
My children Ella, Lola, and Finley have helped me to put this book together. They have guided me as to which recipes are the most fun to make and eat! They have also tested the recipes with the help of some friends, in particular Rosie, Libby, and Tess.

The book has 3 main chapters—Stage 1 (3–5 years), Stage 2 (5–7 years), and Stage 3 (7–11 years). Even though the recipes in Stage 1 are suitable for children aged 3–5 years, if you are older than that and have just picked this book up you can still make the recipes from this section. The recipes in Stage 1 are great for mixing and matching with the other recipes in the book to make a complete meal. For example, crunchy paprika chicken (page 28) is great after pretty shrimp cocktails (page 58) for a special supper, or three fruit salad (page 44) is a lovely dessert to have after pizzas (page 88).

I have included classic favorites like crumble topping (page 76), pastry (page 112), white sauce (page 96), and pizza dough (page 88). This is because I think that these are the basic building blocks for learning to cook. I was fortunate to be taught these recipes by my mother, my grandmother, and my design technology teacher.

There are also lots of other exciting recipes in the book which use some ingredients that we are lucky to find at the store today. You can have a go at making your own sushi (page 102), you can see how to use corn tortillas (page 106), and you can have fun adding herbs and flowers to water to make your own ice bowl (page 70).

Remember that food is expensive, so don't be too disappointed if your parents don't want you to cook every day of the week. But the more you offer to make food that you can all eat as a family, the more likely it is that you will be able to cook, as your parents can include your food in their weekly budget.

THE PHOTOS

The children in the pictures in this book are friends of ours and they came to my kitchen to make the food you see in the photos. Some children asked if they could keep cooking in between having their photos taken, as they were enjoying it so much. For example, while Hector on page 112 was having his photo taken making toffee apple tarts, Sam was making the same tarts in the background because he didn't want to miss out!

YOUR NOTES

As you work your way through a recipe, try to think about it: did you like cooking it and would you like to cook it again? You might like to write some notes in the book. I know that normally you are told not to write in books, but this one is for you to keep forever and you might find it handy to jot down a few comments to remind you of something for next time. For example, would you add more herbs or spice to a recipe? Or make double the amount so that you have enough for friends to share, too?

WHY WE NEED TO EAT

The main reason why we need to eat good food is because it helps us to grow, develop, and stay healthy. Ideally we need to eat 3 meals a day, with 2 small snacks in between. We also need to run around and play sport as much as possible, too, to help keep us fit and healthy.

There are certain types and amounts of food that we need to eat every day. We can eat everything, but we need to eat more of some foods than others. There are 5 main food groups:

1 Bread, rice, potatoes, pasta, and other starchy foods
2 Fruit and vegetables
3 Milk and dairy foods
4 Meat, fish, eggs, beans, and other non-dairy sources of protein
5 Foods and drinks that are high in fat and or sugar

Each day, ideally, we need to eat the following food:

Each meal or snack should contain a food from the bread, cereals, and potatoes section. This means that we eat these foods 5 times a day.
1 portion = a bowl of breakfast cereal or 2 tablespoons of pasta or rice.

Each meal or snack should also contain a fruit or vegetable. We need 5 portions of fresh fruits and vegetables a day.

1 portion = 1 glass of fresh fruit juice, 1 piece of fruit, 2 tablespoons cooked vegetables.

3 portions of milk and dairy foods.
1 portion = 1 small glass of milk, 1 pot of yogurt, 1 tablespoon grated cheese.

1 or 2 portions of meat, fish, and alternatives a day.
1 portion = 2 pink fish fingers (page 60) or an oven-baked herby burger (page 64).

We don't need to eat foods from the fatty and sugary food section every day, as fats and sugars are often found in foods in the other food groups above, but we can have them as treats. Homemade cakes and cookies are good for putting into packed lunches.

Did you know that all the food we eat comes from plants or animals? If possible, try to visit a local farm to see where animals are looked after and where crops are grown.

BEFORE YOU START COOKING

Always ask an adult before you start to make sure that they are happy you are cooking and to check that they will be around to help if you need it.

Try to find all the ingredients and the equipment that you will need for the recipe before you start. Oven mitts are especially important!

You might like to wear an apron. This can help keep the dirt from your clothes falling into the food and also stop the food that you cook going all over your clothes.

Wash your hands before you begin and dry them on a clean towel.

Always try to help clear up after you have made something, and help with the washing and drying up or loading the dishwasher. Your parents are far more likely to let you cook if you don't leave a huge mess behind.

This book is the beginning of your adventure with food and cooking!

11

STAGE 1
3–5 YEARS

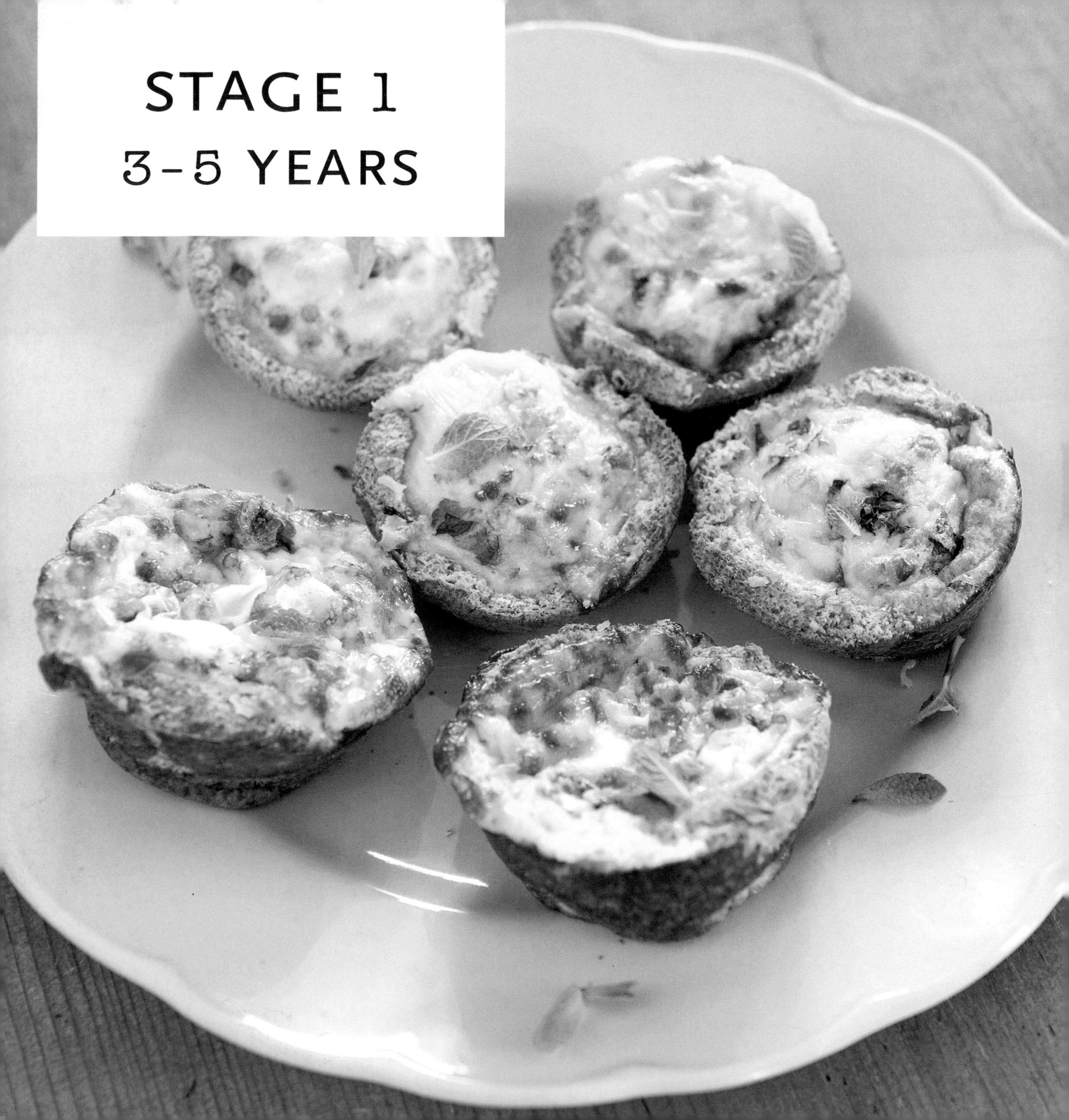

Grownups: this page is for you

CHILDREN: YOU CAN SKIP THIS BIT AND HAVE FUN COOKING!

I am sure you already know this, but I can't stress enough how cooking with children at this stage can have a positive benefit on their development in so many areas. As much as possible, try to let your child complete each step of the recipe on her own to help her to gain a sense of independence in the kitchen.

♦ Cooking will help your child with her physical development, for example her fine motor skills as well as her coordination of movement and eye-hand coordination. Just think about the range of physical skills that she needs to use scissors for cutting fresh herbs, to scoop flour from a container or bag, or to brush melted butter onto dough.

♦ She can measure with spoons and is likely to be able to learn to count. This is why all the ingredients in this section need to be counted or measured with spoons (except for the chocolate kisses).

♦ She will start to work out how to share food evenly, e.g. dividing the fruit between the pies (page 42).

♦ She will start to understand the concept of time, e.g. how long things take to set or cook.

♦ Encouraging your child to cook at this stage can be helpful, as she can make a snack (page 26) or dinner for the family (page 28). She will become more confident with the recipes the more she makes them.

♦ Her attention span will be increasing and she will be able to choose to stop an activity and then come back to it again later.

♦ She will begin to sort things into simple categories, become interested in what causes things to happen, and often ask "why?"

♦ She will begin to be able to understand the concept of "lots" or "a little;" and she will be able to start to recognize primary colors.

♦ She will be able to help find the ingredients or equipment in the kitchen and match them to the pictures in the book.

♦ At this age, children love repetition. She will want to try the new skills over and over again.

♦ She is likely to be starting to enjoy the social element of sitting, talking and eating the food she has made with the rest of the family, and she can start to help with jobs like washing vegetables, and setting and clearing the table.

13

SKILLS

You might find these skills useful for other things that you do (not just cooking), like watering the plants.

USING AN OVEN
Have you ever turned an oven on? Look at the recipe to see what temperature the oven needs to be at and then ask an adult to show you how to set the oven to that temperature. Most ovens have a little light that will go off when the oven has reached the right temperature. **Always use oven mitts when you are putting food in or taking food out of the oven.**

USING A SPOON TO SCOOP
For example, you could try scooping some flour from a big bowl into a little bowl.

STIRRING & MIXING
Try mixing ingredients together with different spoons, for example in the red dip on page 20.

COUNTING
Practice counting the number of spoonfuls or ingredients that you need.

SORTING
Look at the introduction on page 11 of the book to see the different categories of food. You could try sorting basic foods into each category.

SPREADING
Use a table knife to spread something soft like honey or butter onto toast. You will need to gently press the knife onto the food as you spread. Look at pages 26 and 27 for more spreading ideas.

POURING
Use small pitchers that are not too heavy, for pouring liquids from one container to another.

CUTTING WITH A TABLE KNIFE
A table knife is the knife you use to eat your meal with. It is not sharp. Practice cutting something soft like butter or avocado with a table knife.

OPENING & CLOSING JARS
Try opening the lid on a jar. Some jars will be very stiff and you will need some help opening them.

DIPPING
Sometimes you will need to coat a food in a crisp coating to protect the food when it is being cooked and to give it a lovely, crisp texture.

CARRY WITHOUT SPILLING
Practice carrying liquids in containers without spilling them. The first time my son carried his fruit juice pops to the freezer with me when he was three years old we lost half the juice on the way to the freezer, but now we hardly ever have any spillages!

WASHING FRUITS & VEGETABLES
Wash them in a bowl of water or put some water into the sink. It is a good idea to give salad vegetables and root vegetables, like carrots and potatoes that grow underneath the ground, a wash before they are eaten to remove the soil. Mickey had fun washing the vegetables for his dip on page 20.

DRAINING IN A COLANDER
A colander is like a bowl with holes in it. It is useful for draining food like vegetables after you have washed them.

MEASURING WITH SPOONS
The recipes will either say "tablespoon," which is a big spoon or "teaspoon," which is a small spoon. Make sure that you use the right spoon when you are measuring your ingredients.

SHARING
In some recipes you will need to make sure that you share the food evenly, like sharing the fillings between tarts. You don't want all of the filling in some of the tarts and none in the others!

FREEZING
Freezers were invented to help keep food fresh for a long time without it going bad. How does food freeze? Most food contains lots of water. Freezing works by changing this water to ice. Put a liquid into a freezer and watch it change to a solid. The solid is called ice. See page 39 for fruit juice pops.

TOUCHING FOOD
When you touch food, think about how it feels—is it cold, slimy, hard, or soft? On page 28 Lara loved touching the cold chicken and dipping it in the soft tomato purée and then the crunchy crackers. Just remember never to lick your fingers after you have touched raw meat or fish.

MASHING
This is when you squash food using a potato masher, fork, or mortar and pestle. Practice with soft fruits, e.g. page 36, or garlic, e.g. page 18.

TEARING
Try tearing some fresh herbs or lettuce leaves and then smelling them. My children like to smell mint, as they think it smells like toothpaste!

HULLING STRAWBERRIES
Use your fingers to pull the green stalks off the top of strawberries. You might need to dig your fingers into the fruit slightly so that you pull out the hard bit where the fruit and the stalk meet.

CUTTING WITH COOKIE CUTTERS
Press the cutter into bread or pastry and twist it slightly to make sure that it cuts all the way through, and then lift the cutter up.

CUTTING WITH SCISSORS
Always make sure that your fingers stay away from the scissors so that you don't cut them accidentally.

BRUSHING
Use a pastry brush to brush milk, melted butter, or oil. For example, brushing oil onto baking sheets helps to stop the food from sticking to the sheets.

ROLLING
Use a rolling pin to flatten something like bread (see page 22) or pastry (see page 42). When you roll pastry, try to roll small pieces of pastry, one at a time; it is much easier than rolling one big piece. Push the rolling pin down onto the pastry and roll it away from you.

SHAPING
Use your hands to mold the food into a shape. For example, for the strawberry candy (page 38), you will need to mold the dough to make strawberry shapes. For the chocolate kisses (page 46), you need to mold the dough into small balls.

BASHING WITH A PESTLE
You don't have to have one of these, but if you do, try bashing a peeled clove of garlic to make the salad dressing on page 18.

CRUSHING GARLIC
Garlic grows in a "bulb" with lots of small "cloves" inside. Before you crush a clove of garlic you will need to peel it to remove the papery skin. Dig a fingernail into the skin to break it, then pull the skin away. To crush the clove put it in a garlic press and squeeze the press to close. You may need to scrape the crushed garlic off the press with a table knife. If you don't have a press, just bash the garlic with a rolling pin to release some of its juices and flavor and keep it whole.

SETTING THE TABLE
Have fun setting the table and clearing away. The fork sits on the left of the plate and the knife on the right. The knife blade faces towards the plate.

TASTING NEW FOODS
Try something new—you might like it. You will also need to taste the food that you have made to check that it tastes good before other people try it. Use a teaspoon to taste your food.

KITCHEN EQUIPMENT

These are a few things that you might find useful to have in the kitchen, however you don't need them all to do some cooking.

ROLLING PIN
These come in all different sizes, they are easy to use and great fun. They are needed for rolling out dough or bread and they can be used for bashing olives to help remove their stones and bashing garlic cloves to help remove their skins!

CUTTERS
These come in all different shapes and sizes. Have fun cutting out circles of bread for the tasty bread tarts (page 34).

STRAINER
Why do we need to use a strainer? To remove any lumps and to add air so that the food we cook or bake is light.

MIXING SPOONS
Wooden and melamine spoons are both great for mixing ingredients together.

PASTRY BRUSH
This is useful for brushing melted butter onto pastry, like the mini fruit pies on page 42 or for brushing oil onto baking sheets e.g. the burgers on page 64 (if you are not using parchment paper).

PESTLE & MORTAR
You don't need one of these but they are fun to use for bashing food like cloves of garlic to make a dressing for a salad like on page 18. If you don't have one you can use a small rolling pin and a little bowl instead. The pestle is the stick and the mortar is the name given to the bowl.

POTATO MASHER OR FORK
This is for mashing soft fruit and vegetables.

MELON BALLER
If you don't have one of these, you can use a small teaspoon instead.

GARLIC PRESS
Peel the garlic clove first and then put the clove inside the garlic press. Push down to squeeze the garlic out (see page 15, above).

CUTTING BOARD
Always wash your cutting board after you have used it. This is very important if you have used it to cut meat, poultry, or fish.

MUFFIN PAN
You need this for the bread tarts on page 34 and you can also use it to make small cakes.

BAKING SHEET
These are very handy. For example, you will need one for the DIY pizzas on page 32, and many other things which you cook in the oven.

MIXING BOWL
These come in all different shapes and sizes. They are useful for so many different recipes, whether you are making a cake or mixing leaves together to make a salad.

COLANDER
This is like a strainer but it has bigger holes. It is great for draining things like cooked pasta or a jar of olives.

WIRE COOLING RACK
You don't have to have one of these, but it is useful for helping food to cool down.

CLEAR MEASURING CUPS
Available in 1-, 2-, and 4-cup sizes, use these for measuring liquids. The spout makes it easy to carefully pour a liquid.

FORK, TABLE KNIFE, SPOON
This is the cutlery that you use to eat with.

BIG & SMALL BOWL, PLATE
Hopefully this will not be too difficult to find in your kitchen cupboards.

OVEN
There are so many different types of ovens. Ask your parents to show you how yours works. Most ovens have a little light on them which will go off when the oven has reached the right temperature.

OVEN MITTS
You can't cook safely without these. Whenever you help to put anything in or take anything out of the oven you must always put your oven mitts on! It is very easy to burn yourself.

SCISSORS
If you don't have kitchen scissors, use paper scissors to snip herbs but make sure that you wash them before and after you use them to cut up food. When you use scissors, always keep your fingers away from the blades so that you don't accidentally cut yourself.

MEASURING SPOONS
You will need 2 different sizes of spoon for recipes: a "tablespoon," which is a big spoon and a "teaspoon," which is a small spoon. Make sure that you use the right spoon when you are measuring your ingredients.

salad bar with Susan's dressing

This is a recipe for a salad dressing. It is very useful to know how to make a good dressing so that you can always enjoy eating yummy salads. My friend Susan makes the best salad dressing and it tastes just like this. It is my children's idea to make a "salad bar." They like to choose salad ingredients from the fridge, put them into bowls and then we all help ourselves. Sometimes they choose things like grated carrot, corn kernels, and crunchy bread croutons to go with the salad greens.

SKILLS
- USING MORTAR & PESTLE
- MEASURING WITH SPOONS
- MIXING
- CUTTING WITH TABLE KNIFE
- WASHING
- POURING

1 To make Susan's dressing, peel the thin, pink skin away from the garlic clove and if you have a mortar and pestle, put the garlic into the bowl, add a tiny pinch of salt,** and bash the garlic until you have a paste. If you don't have a mortar and pestle, crush the garlic in a garlic press and put into a small pitcher, then use a small whisk to whisk everything together.

2 Add the mustard, balsamic vinegar and white wine vinegar and a little freshly ground black pepper and mix again.
3 Add the olive oil a little at a time—keep mixing all the time so that you end up with a smooth dressing. This will come with practice. Keep making it every time you have a salad!

For 4 people you need:

SUSAN'S DRESSING

1 garlic clove
tiny pinch of salt**
1 teaspoon mustard (English, whole-grain or Dijon are all fine)
1 teaspoon balsamic vinegar
1 tablespoon white wine vinegar
a little freshly ground black pepper
6 tablespoons olive oil

SALAD INGREDIENTS

You can use any salad ingredients that you like. Here are some that we often use:
ripe avocado* and cooked, peeled fresh beets (you can chop these using a table knife)
salad greens e.g. lettuce leaves, arugula, watercress, baby spinach leaves
cherry tomatoes, pitted olives, pine nuts, small mozzarella balls

EQUIPMENT

mortar and pestle • table knife
cutting board • several small bowls
colander • clean kitchen towel • small pitcher

4 If you have some soft foods, like avocado* or beets, you might like to cut these into small pieces using a table knife and then put them into bowls.

5 Wash the lettuce in a colander in the sink, then shake or dry with a clean kitchen towel. Put the lettuce in a bowl and then put all your other salad ingredients into small bowls. Pour your dressing into a small pitcher. Let everyone help themselves to the pick 'n' mix salad bar. You will have some salad dressing left over to use another day. Keep it in a clean jar in the fridge.

* Please ask an adult or older child to cut the avocado in half.
** I don't add salt to any recipes for children, but this is an exception, as the salt helps you to mash the garlic to a paste.

STAGE
1

red dip
with crunchy veggies

Parents seem to like this dip just as much as the children do and it's a great way to try different vegetables, too. You could also make some tortilla chips from page 30 to eat with the dip. Mickey had great fun making this.

For 2–3 people you need:

INGREDIENTS
2 tablespoons tomato ketchup
4 tablespoons cream cheese
2 handfuls each: sugar snap peas, baby corn, small carrots and cherry tomatoes

EQUIPMENT
spoon • mixing bowl • bowl of water clean kitchen towel • small bowl • plate

1 Count the spoons of tomato ketchup into a mixing bowl and then spoon the cream cheese into the bowl. You might need a small spoon to scrape the cream cheese from the big spoon. Mix to make an orangey-red mixture.
2 Wash the vegetables—put them in a bowl of water and wipe with your hands to get rid of any dirt or grit. If you clean the carrots really well, you won't need to peel them. Gently shake the vegetables to dry them or spread them on a clean kitchen towel to dry out.
3 Spoon the red dip into a small bowl and put it on a plate. Count the dry vegetables as you place them on the plate next to the dip. Now dip the vegetables into the dip and enjoy eating!

SKILLS
◆ WASHING
VEGETABLES
◆ USING SPOON
◆ COUNTING
◆ MIXING
◆ DIPPING

STAGE
1

roly-poly sandwich

Use a little smoked salmon as a treat in this sandwich, or you could use ham or salami instead. Try different types of bread like whole-wheat, white, or multigrain. Have a look in your local bakery or supermarket at all the different kinds. If you have had fun making these sandwiches, you might like to try the Super Sushi Rolls on page 102, which are also rolled into pretty spiral shapes.

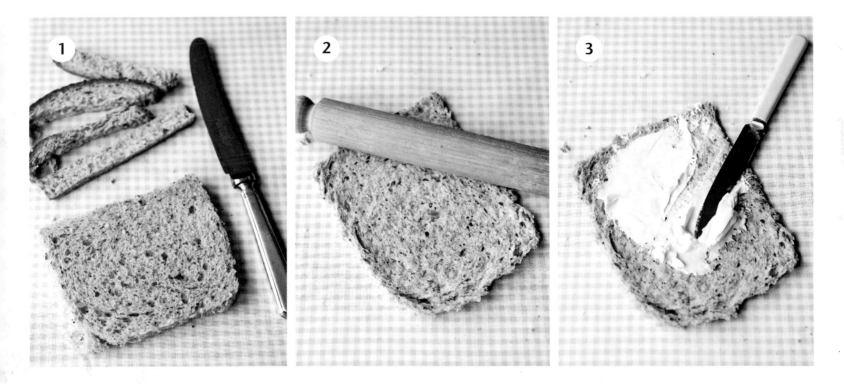

1 Put the slice of bread on a clean surface and use a table knife to cut the crusts off.
2 Flatten the slice of bread by rolling over it with a rolling pin.
3 Spread the cream cheese onto the bread with the table knife.
4 Lay the smoked salmon on top of the cream cheese and then sprinkle the mustard and cress over the salmon.
5 Starting with a short side of the bread slice, roll the bread up into a long sausage shape.

Cut the sausage shape with the table knife into 5 roly-poly sandwiches. When you lay them flat on a plate you'll see that you have made spirals!

Other filling ideas
A little canned salmon or tuna, drained and mashed with a fork, mixed with a little mayonnaise, then scattered with a few torn lettuce or spinach leaves over the top. Or grated hard cheese, ham torn into very small pieces, and a finely chopped tomato.

For 1 roly-poly sandwich you need:

INGREDIENTS
1 slice whole-wheat, white, or
multigrain bread
1 tablespoon cream cheese
2 slices smoked salmon
a little mustard and cress

EQUIPMENT
table knife ◆ *rolling pin* ◆ *small plate*

SKILLS
◆ SPREADING
◆ ROLLING
◆ CUTTING WITH TABLE KNIFE

cheesy stuffed peppers

You need to choose small sweet bell peppers from a greengrocer or a large supermarket for this recipe. These cheesy stuffed peppers are easy to make and eat and are great with some crusty bread for a packed lunch or a quick snack. Don't forget to smell the herbs as you spend some time choosing which ones to add to your cream cheese mixture. Maya made 5 stuffed peppers.

SKILLS MIXING ◆ SPOONING ◆ SMELLING HERBS

For 1 mini pepper you need:

INGREDIENTS
1 mini sweet bell pepper, top cut off (please ask an adult or older child to do this)
about 1 tablespoon cream cheese
2 teaspoons plain yogurt
a few fresh herb leaves e.g. dill, thyme, sage, or parsley

EQUIPMENT
mixing bowl ◆ spoon ◆ scissors

1 Use your fingers to scrape the little seeds out of the mini bell pepper.
2 Put the cream cheese and yogurt in a mixing bowl and mix together with a spoon.

3 Pick the leaves off some herbs, or using scissors, snip the herb leaves into small pieces and add to the cream cheese mixture. Stir with the spoon. Spoon the cheese mixture into the pepper and put the lid back on top.

ants on a log

This is a quick and easy snack that you can make all by yourself. It's also a good way to practice spreading, which will be useful when you make your own sandwiches and put jam or honey on your toast for breakfast.

For 2 celery boats you need:

INGREDIENTS
1 celery rib, cut in half
a little peanut butter
10 dried cranberries, raisins, or other dried fruit

EQUIPMENT
bowl of water • clean kitchen towel table knife

1 Wash the celery—put it in a bowl of water and wipe with your hands to get rid of any dirt or grit. Gently shake the celery to dry it or dry it with a clean kitchen towel.
2 Use a table knife to spread some peanut butter into the celery stick pieces.
3 Count 5 dried fruits and stick them onto the peanut butter.

SKILLS
◆ WASHING VEGETABLES
◆ SPREADING
◆ COUNTING

cucumber snacks

For an extra-quick snack you could try spreading some cream cheese onto cucumber slices and decorating them with pieces of dried apricot to make them look a bit like buttons. They taste yummy too!

For 4 buttons you need:

INGREDIENTS
4 slices cucumber
1 tablespoon cream cheese
1 dried apricot

EQUIPMENT
table knife • scissors

1 Use a table knife to spread a little cream cheese on top of each cucumber slice.
2 Using scissors, snip the dried apricots into small pieces.
3 Dot the apricot pieces over the cream cheese, counting them as you go: how many pieces have you added?

SKILLS
◆ SPREADING
◆ COUNTING
◆ USING SCISSORS

STAGE
1

crunchy paprika chicken

Try this crispy chicken with different coatings, such as crunchy crackers for cheese or bread crumbs; my children like to dip the chicken into cornflakes (instead of crackers) too.

For 4 people you need:

INGREDIENTS

about 10 whole-grain crackers
(or 10 tablespoons cornflakes)
1 large pinch paprika
4 tablespoons tomato paste (or ketchup)
4 free-range skinless chicken thigh fillets, already cut into pieces (about 14 oz.)
salad and boiled new potatoes go well with the chicken

EQUIPMENT

scissors ◆ parchment paper ◆ 2 baking sheets
2 mixing bowls ◆ spoon ◆ oven mitts

1 Turn the oven on to 350°F. Cut 2 pieces of parchment paper, each big enough to cover the baking sheets, or brush a little olive oil over the sheets. Count the crackers into a mixing bowl and use your fingers to crush them into very small pieces. Add the paprika to the bowl, too, and mix with your hands.
2 Count the 4 spoonfuls of tomato paste and put them into another bowl.
3 Dip the chicken pieces into the tomato paste so that there is a bit of paste all over every piece.
4 Dip the pieces of chicken into the crushed crackers so that the cracker pieces stick to the chicken.
5 Put the crunchy chicken straight onto the lined baking sheets. Now, WASH YOUR HANDS—you must always wash your hands thoroughly after handling raw meat.
6 Ask an adult to help you put the sheets into the oven using oven mitts. Cook for 20 minutes or until the chicken is golden brown and cooked all the way through—ask an adult to help you check this.

SKILLS
- ◆ CRUSHING
- ◆ COUNTING
- ◆ DIPPING
- ◆ USING OVEN

STAGE
1

green dip with tortilla chips

When you have friends you could have this as an appetizer instead of having a dessert. My son Finley and I created the tortilla chips when we found some slightly stale corn tortillas in the cupboard. He suggested that we cut them up and make them into chips like we sometimes do with pita bread, so we did. They taste good!

SKILLS
- USING SCISSORS
- USING MORTAR & PESTLE
- USING TEASPOON
- MASHING

1 Turn the oven on to 350°F. Using scissors, snip the corn tortillas into small pieces and put on a baking sheet. Ask an adult to help you put the sheet into the oven using oven mitts. Bake for 5 minutes until golden and starting to crisp. Ask an adult to help you take the chips out of the oven.
2 Peel the garlic (see page 88 for help). If you have a mortar and pestle, put the garlic into the mortar (bowl) and bash with the pestle until you have a paste. If you don't have a mortar and pestle, use the end of a small rolling pin and a bowl.

Using scissors, snip the cilantro into small pieces.
3 Add the cilantro to the mortar (or bowl). Squeeze the juice from the lime half into the mortar. Mash with the pestle.
4 Scoop the pits out of the avocados with a teaspoon and peel away the skins.
5 Add some of the avocado flesh to the mortar and mash. Add the rest of the avocado flesh and mash again until you have a lumpy paste. Spoon the dip into a small bowl and serve with the chips.
* Please ask an adult or older child to cut the avocados in half.

For 4 people you need:
INGREDIENTS
4 corn tortillas
1 garlic clove
handful cilantro leaves
½ lime
2 ripe avocados, cut in half*
EQUIPMENT
*scissors • baking sheet • oven mitts
mortar and pestle • spoon • small bowl*

4

5

STAGE
1

DIY pizzas

This is one of my son Finley's favorite lunches which he has been making since he was three—the same age as Sholto in these pictures. I am a big fan of making pizzas using flour tortillas, English muffins, or French bread as they are quick and you can use any topping ingredients you have in the kitchen. My eldest daughter has even cooked these on a campfire—roll the tortilla up into a sausage first, wrap in foil, and ask an adult to put it on the fire for 10 minutes.

To make 4 pizzas you need:

INGREDIENTS

4 flour tortillas, pieces French bread, halved English muffins or rolls
8 teaspoons canned tomato purée or chopped tomatoes for each pizza
your choice of toppings (these are a few of our favorites):
grated cheese, canned tuna, pitted olives, corn kernels, pieces ham or salami, sliced bell pepper, sliced mushrooms, sliced cherry tomatoes

EQUIPMENT

scissors • parchment paper 2 baking sheets • spoon oven mitts • cutting board table knife

1 Turn the oven on to 400°F. Cut 2 pieces of parchment paper, each big enough to cover the baking sheets. Put 2 tortillas on each baking sheet.

2 Count 6 teaspoons of tomato purée onto each tortilla.

3 Use the back of the spoon to spread the tomatoes over the tortillas but leave a little border around the edge so that it doesn't drip over the edges when the pizza is in the oven.

4 Choose some toppings and sprinkle them over the tomatoes. Ask an adult to help you put the baking sheets into the oven using oven mitts. Bake for 5 minutes. Ask an adult to help you take the cooked pizzas out of the oven using oven mitts and put them onto a cutting board. Using a table knife, cut them in half, then in half again to make quarters. Sholto liked to cut his pizza into quarters on his own and he said that it tasted very good.

SKILLS
- ◆ SPREADING
- ◆ CHOOSING TOPPINGS
- ◆ CUTTING WITH TABLE KNIFE
- ◆ USING OVEN

STAGE 1

tasty bread tarts

It can be frustrating if you want to cook something but you don't have the ingredients to do it. These tarts use basic ingredients that you should find in your kitchen like bread, milk, and eggs. You can add other fillings like corn and tuna.

To make 6 tarts you need:

INGREDIENTS
a little unsalted butter
6 slices multigrain bread
3 free-range eggs and 4 tablespoons milk (or 2 eggs and 6 tablespoons milk)
handful fresh mint leaves (or other herbs) —have you ever smelt fresh mint leaves? They smell amazing!
2 handfuls frozen (and defrosted) or fresh peas or corn kernels
small handful grated Parmesan

EQUIPMENT
scrap of parchment paper • muffin pan round cutter as wide as the slices of bread cutting board • oven mitts • table knife small pitcher • spoon • fork • scissors

1 Turn the oven on to 375°F. Take the round cutter and press it into each slice of bread on a cutting board to cut out 6 circles.

2 Using a scrap of parchment paper, rub some butter inside 6 of the holes in the muffin pan. Press each bread circle into the buttered muffin pan holes. Ask an adult to help you put the muffin pan into the oven using oven mitts. Bake for 5 minutes. Ask an adult to help you take the muffin pan out of the oven using oven mitts and let cool.

3 Now you need to crack open the eggs: hold an egg in one hand and carefully use a table knife to crack the egg in the middle. Put your thumbs into the crack and pull the egg shell apart. Let the egg fall into a small pitcher. Repeat with the other eggs. (See page 60 for a photo of how to crack eggs.) Mix the eggs with a fork to break them up. Add the milk and mix the milk and eggs together with a fork again.

5

6

4 Using scissors, snip the mint into small pieces and put a little into each tart. Now put a few peas into each tart too—try to share them out evenly so that the tarts have roughly the same amount.

5 Slowly pour the egg mixture that's in the pitcher into the tarts over the peas and mint—try to stop pouring just before you reach the top, as the tarts will rise in the oven.

6 Sprinkle a little grated Parmesan over the tarts. Ask an adult to help you put the muffin pan back in the oven using oven mitts. Cook for 12 minutes, or until they have puffed up and the egg is cooked.

SKILLS ◆ CUTTING SHAPES WITH CUTTERS AND SHARING TOPPINGS BETWEEN THE CASES.
◆ I HAVE ALSO SHOWN YOU HOW TO CRACK EGGS, WHICH IS IN THE NEXT SECTION OF THE BOOK, BUT YOU MIGHT LIKE TO START PRACTICING THIS SKILL NOW. DON'T WORRY IF SOME SHELL FALLS IN WITH THE EGG —JUST FISH IT OUT WITH A SPOON.

STAGE
1

fizzy strawberry crush

This is great for practicing mashing fruit and pouring from a glass measuring cup. This drink is made with fizzy water, so you need to drink it straightaway before the bubbles disappear. If you don't like fizz, just add more fruit juice instead.

To make 2 glasses you need:

INGREDIENTS
2 large handfuls ripe strawberries
orange juice to half fill your glasses
fizzy water (or if you don't want fizz, add more juice or still water)

EQUIPMENT
bowl ◆ potato masher ◆ spoon ◆ glass measuring cup ◆ 2 glasses

1 Hull the strawberries—this means to pull the green stalks off the tops. You might need to dig your fingers into the strawberries to really pull the tops out.
2 Put the strawberries into a bowl and mash with a potato masher.
3 Spoon the strawberries into a glass measuring cup.
4 Pour the orange juice onto the strawberries and mix with a spoon.
5 Pour the fizzy water into the cup, too and mix again with the spoon.
6 Pour the drink into 2 glasses. Drink right away! If you haven't had a fizzy drink before, you might find that the bubbles feel funny in your mouth.

SKILLS
◆ HULLING STRAWBERRIES
◆ MASHING
◆ SPOONING
◆ POURING

5

6

Lola's strawberry candy

Lola, my middle daughter, came up with this sweet idea. Even though these are quick to make, you will need to have some patience and wait for the candy to dry after you have made it. This is just like playing with play dough!

SKILLS
- MASHING
- MAKING DOUGH
- SHAPING
- USING SCISSORS

To make about 20 strawberries you need:

INGREDIENTS
1 ripe strawberry (eat some more fresh strawberries while you're waiting for the sweets to set!)
1 tablespoon cream cheese
½ capful vanilla extract
about 2 cups confectioners' sugar (you may need slightly more or less)
long thin green candies to make strawberry "stalks"

EQUIPMENT
mixing bowl • fork • parchment paper plate • scissors • pretty serving plate

1 Hull the strawberry—this means to pull the green stalk off the top using your fingers. Put the strawberry, cream cheese, and vanilla into a mixing bowl and mash with a fork.

2 Add 3 spoonfuls of the confectioners' sugar to the bowl and mix again. Add 3 more spoonfuls and keep mixing. You might want to use your hands now to mix. Keep adding sugar until you have a firm dough that is not too sticky.

3 Take a small piece of the mixture—about the size of a real strawberry—and shape it into a ball. Now squash it into a strawberry shape and put onto a plate. (You might like to put a piece of parchment paper on the plate first so that the candies don't stick to the plate.) Take the fork and push it into the candy to make holes. Repeat for the rest of the candies.

4 Using scissors, cut the green candies into short pieces, then cut a few slits into each piece so that they fan open to look like leaves. Push into the strawberry candies and let dry for 3–4 hours. Transfer them to a pretty plate before you serve them!

stripey fruit juice pops

This is a great way to learn about freezing and watching liquid change to a solid. You can use old yogurt tubs or plastic cups, and wooden popsicle sticks or plastic spoons. Don't use metal spoons as they will be too cold to hold when they freeze.

To make as many as you like you need:

INGREDIENTS
purple fruit juice (I used blackcurrant but you could also try a red fruit juice like raspberry)
apple juice

EQUIPMENT
old yogurt tubs and the same number of wooden popsicle sticks or plastic spoons (or lolly molds) • you will also need to make sure there is room in your freezer to stand all your yogurt tubs or lolly molds

1 Find some old yogurt tubs and make sure that they are clean and dry. You will also need some wooden popsicle sticks or plastic spoons—you should have enough of these to go in all your yogurt tubs. Put one popsicle stick or spoon into each yogurt tub. Start pouring the purple fruit juice into a yogurt tub until it's half full. Repeat this with all your other yogurt tubs. You might like to pour the purple juice first into some of the tubs and the apple juice first into the other tubs so that the stripes look different when the pops are frozen.

2 Put the tubs into the freezer and freeze until frozen—this will take at least 4 hours. Take the tubs out of the freezer and pour the other juice over the frozen juice until you nearly reach the top of the tub. Don't fill them too full!

3 Put the tubs back into the freezer and freeze again for 4 hours or until you have frozen ice pops. When you take the pops out of the freezer, you might need to sit each one in a little warm water to help ease the pop itself out of the tub, but don't let it sit in the warm water for long otherwise it will melt.

STAGE
1

berry crunch

This is like a fruit smoothie but with some crunch added. It makes a wonderful breakfast, dessert, or snack. The amounts in this recipe are only a guide, as the exact quantities will vary depending on the size of glasses that you decide to use.

For 2 glasses you need:

INGREDIENTS
4 handfuls fresh berries
4 tablespoons plain Greek yogurt
8 tablespoons crunchy cereal or muesli

EQUIPMENT
bowl ◆ fork ◆ spoon ◆ 2 glasses

1 Put most of the berries into a bowl (save a few for decorating the top) and mash with a fork or potato masher.
2 Count the spoons of yogurt into the bowl with the mashed berries and mix with the spoon.
3 Spoon a bit of the cereal into the bottom of the glasses and spoon the fruity yogurt on top of the cereal. You will start to see layers in the glasses.

Spoon a little more cereal on top of the yogurt and then dollop some more yogurt on top of the cereal. Finish with the saved berries on top.

SKILLS
◆ MASHING
◆ SPOONING
◆ MIXING

mini fruit pies

Ready-made puff pastry dough is just right for these mini fruit pies. When you are rolling dough, it is much easier to roll one small piece at a time instead of rolling one large piece, which is why I have broken the pastry into 4 pieces. These pastries taste delicious and are good for packed lunches, at snack time, or for desserts. If you choose to use big dried fruits like mango or apricots, you will need to use scissors to cut them into small pieces first.

1 Turn the oven on to 350°F. Cut a piece of parchment paper big enough to cover the baking sheet. Put the melted butter, dried fruits, and spice in a mixing bowl and mix with a spoon.

2 Break the dough in half, then break each piece in half to make 4 pieces. Sprinkle a little flour on the work surface. Flatten one piece of dough with a rolling pin until it is about the same thickness as 2 stacked pennies.

3 Take the cutter and, starting at the edge of the dough, push it down to cut out circles. Keep going until you have used up all of that dough. Roll out another piece of dough and cut out circles. Repeat with the rest of the dough. Using a teaspoon, spoon a little fruit mixture onto the middle of each circle. Bring the edges of the circle up together to seal the mixture inside. There should be no gaps in the pastry!

4 Turn the parcels over and flatten slightly with your hand. Using a table knife, carefully cut 2 or 3 short slits in the top of each pastry—this will let the steam escape when the pastries are baking.

5 Put them on the baking sheet. Dip a pastry brush in a little melted butter and brush over all the pies. Sprinkle with sugar. Ask an adult to help you put the sheet in the oven and bake for 15 minutes. They should look golden!

To make 16 mini pies you need:

INGREDIENTS

small piece of butter, about the size
of 2 pieces of chocolate, melted
(ask an adult or older child to do
this), plus a little extra
20 tablespoons (1⅓ cups) dried fruits
1 teaspoon mixed spice
12½ oz. puff pastry dough
a little flour for sprinkling
a little demerara sugar for sprinkling

EQUIPMENT

*scissors • parchment paper • baking
sheet • mixing bowl • spoon • rolling
pin • 2 pennies • round cutter about
2¼ inches across • spoon • table knife
pastry brush*

SKILLS

◆ MIXING
◆ ROLLING PASTRY
◆ CUTTING CIRCLES
◆ BRUSHING
◆ USING OVEN

three fruit salad

Have you ever made melon balls before? It's great fun scooping the melon flesh into balls. A melon baller doesn't cost very much to buy —just look in any good kitchen store. If you don't have a melon baller, you can use a small teaspoon. You can make a fruit salad with other fruits as well, like strawberries, raspberries, and sliced peaches. It's tasty, colorful, and good for you, too!

For 3 people you need:

INGREDIENTS
½ ripe melon (seeds removed)
2 tangerines
1 ripe banana
⅔ cup orange and mango juice
(or other juice of your choice)

EQUIPMENT
melon baller or small rounded teaspoon
pretty bowl • table knife • spoon

1 Use a melon baller or a teaspoon to scoop out small balls of melon flesh and put into a pretty bowl for the fruit salad.
2 Peel the tangerines and then, using a table knife, cut each segment in half. Add to the bowl of melon balls.
3 Peel the banana.

4 Using the table knife again, cut the banana into small pieces. Add to the bowl.
5 Pour the juice over the fruit and stir together.

SKILLS
◆ USING MELON BALLER
◆ POURING

44

4

5

chocolate kisses

This is the first recipe in the book that needs the ingredients to be weighed. There is more information about weighing in Stage 2 of the book. If you weigh everything before you start cooking, the rest is very easy.

To make 25 kisses you need:

INGREDIENTS

1 stick plus 5 tablespoons unsalted butter, soft
½ cup natural cane sugar or granulated sugar
capful vanilla extract
2 cups self-rising flour
2 tablespoons cocoa powder

RASPBERRY CREAM

4 ripe raspberries
6½ tablespoons unsalted butter, soft
⅔ cup confectioners' sugar

EQUIPMENT

scrap of paper ◆ 2 baking sheets ◆ mixing bowl
wooden spoon ◆ oven mitts ◆ small bowl ◆ fork

1 Turn the oven on to 350°F. Take a scrap of paper and use it to rub a little butter over 2 baking sheets.
2 Put the soft butter, sugar, and vanilla extract in a mixing bowl and mix well with a wooden spoon until it becomes fluffy and paler in color. This helps to beat air into the mixture.
3 Tip the flour and cocoa powder into the bowl and mix well with your hands.
4 Break the mixture into 5. Now break each piece into 10 pieces, all the same size. Roll each piece into small balls about the size of a small walnut, then flatten a bit. Put onto the baking sheets and ask an adult to help you put them in the oven using oven mitts. Bake for 6–7 minutes, then ask an adult to help you take the sheets out of the oven. Let cool.
5 For the raspberry cream, put the berries into a small bowl, mash with a fork, then add the butter and sugar and mix with the fork.
6 Spoon a little cream onto a kiss and sandwich with another kiss. Keep going until you have 25 kisses.

SKILLS

◆ BUTTERING BAKING SHEETS
◆ INTRODUCTION TO CREAMING BUTTER AND SUGAR (SEE PAGE 51)
◆ SHAPING
◆ MASHING

STAGE 2
5–7 YEARS

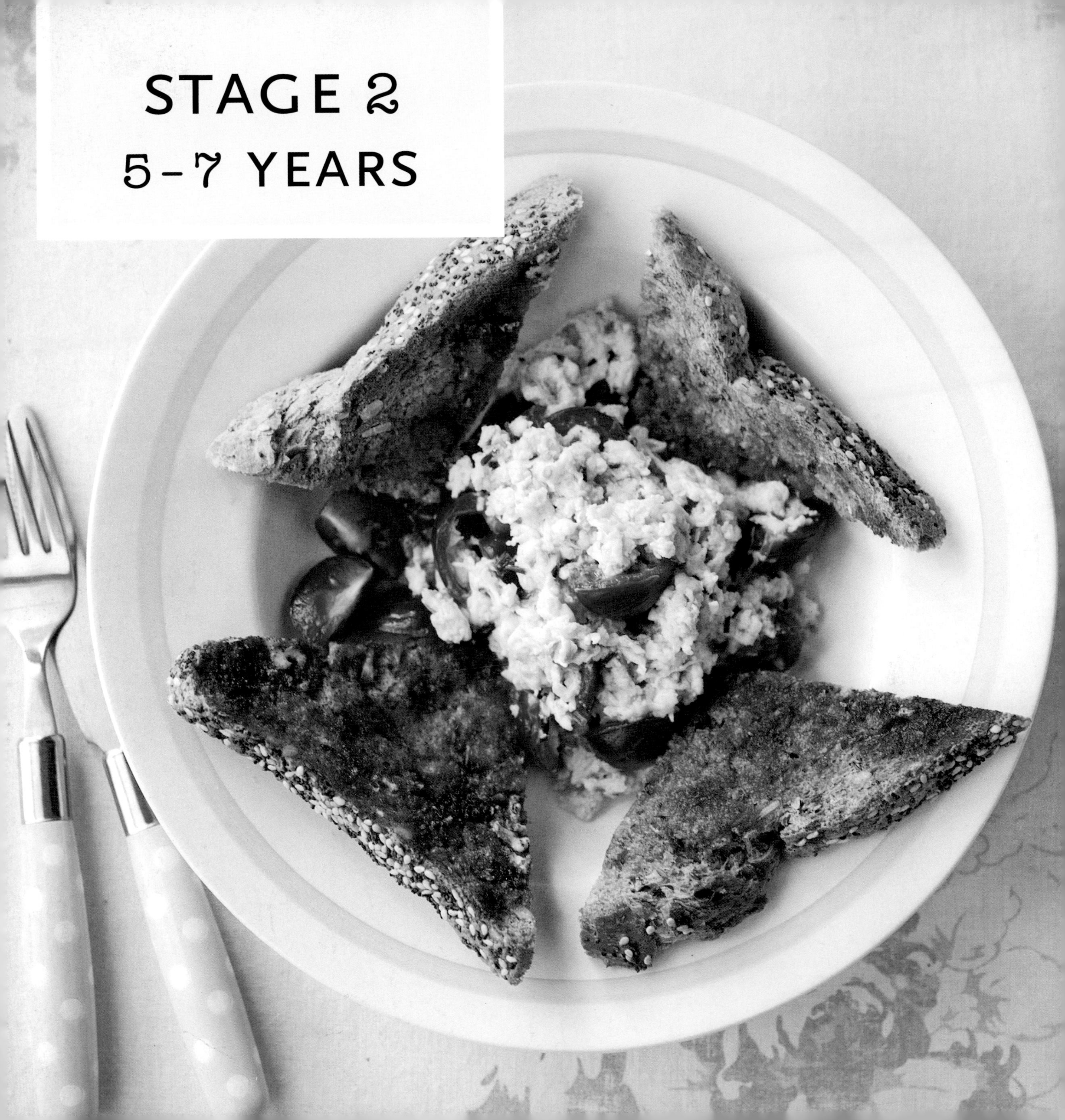

Grownups: this page is for you

CHILDREN: YOU CAN SKIP THIS BIT AND HAVE FUN COOKING!

As your child works through these recipes, help him to link them up with recipes and skills from the previous chapter. He could make the red dip as a starter (page 20), then the oven-baked herby burgers from this chapter for the entrée.

♦ At some point during this stage, he is likely to be ready to learn how to use a small, sharp knife for cutting, but make sure that you always stay with him and guide him to follow safe cutting techniques.

♦ Your child will be more aware of size, shape, and weight. Encourage him to guess the weights of random objects and then weigh them to see what the result is. Also encourage him to measure all the ingredients for a recipe before he starts cooking.

♦ He will be growing toward reading and writing independently. Encourage him to read some of the words and to follow the sequence of steps for the recipes with the photos to guide him.

♦ He will be more willing to work out what he needs to do next, so try to avoid the temptation to tell him. As much as possible, let him work through recipes on his own.

♦ He will be more expressive with his language and more willing to share what he thinks of a recipe. After he has made something, ask him about it, e.g. if he would change anything if he made it again.

♦ He will start to show an interest in the science behind food and will enjoy watching food like couscous change from small, inedible hard pellets to something soft that is good to eat.

♦ He will be ready to use more complex kitchen equipment, like graters or lemon juicers.

♦ Encourage him to use his imagination by adding his own ingredients e.g. other toppings to the tomato tarts on page 56.

♦ He will be able to help work out how long the food needs to cook in the oven and how to share the food evenly between the whole family.

♦ He will have an increased interest in the world around him and where food comes from. Help him to understand that all the food we eat comes from plants and animals and that some of these plants grow in other countries.

♦ He will want to help with simple tasks like setting and clearing the table, and this will help with his social development.

SKILLS

I hope that you enjoyed learning the skills in Stage 1. Here are some more to have fun practicing as you cook some new recipes.

USING A BROILER

Does your oven have a broiler? Most ovens do. When you turn it on, the element will heat up until it is red. If you put some food underneath the broiler, like the bagel on page 66, the broiler will toast it until it is golden and bubbling. **Always use oven mitts when you are putting food under or removing food from the broiler.**

KNIVES

Always ask an adult before you use a sharp knife. It is likely that you will be ready now, with help from an adult, to use a small paring knife. The safest and most popular ways to use a knife are the bridge-cutting and claw-cutting techniques.

BRIDGE-CUTTING TECHNIQUE

Hold the food between a thumb and finger of one hand to make a bridge. Hold a small paring knife in the other hand, put the blade under the bridge and cut downward through the food.

CLAW-CUTTING TECHNIQUE

Make your fingers into a "claw" shape, tucking your thumb inside your fingers. Use this claw to hold the food. Hold a small paring knife in your other hand and cut the food. As the knife moves along the food, pull the claw away from the knife.

GRATING

Hold the handle of the grater with one hand and then push the cheese downward over the grater "teeth." Always keep your fingers away from the grater "teeth," as they are very sharp.

LINING A BAKING PAN

You will need to sit the pan on the paper first and draw around it before you cut it with scissors. If you do this, the paper should fit inside the pan.

MEASURING

Have you ever measured a liquid before? Fill a pitcher with water. You will then need a glass measuring cup: this is a clear glass pitcher with measurements written up the side. Carefully pour water into the measuring cup, up to the level that you need e.g. ½ cup.

MEASURING VOLUME

If you want to work out the "volume" of a container (that is how much liquid the container will hold), first fill it with water, then pour this water into a glass measuring cup. Write down the level on the measuring cup on a piece of paper. You then know how much liquid you need to fill the container. You could practice this by making some stripey frozen fruit pops (see page 39).

WEIGHING

Learn how to use a scale. All scales are different, so you will need to ask an adult to show you how to use yours. Why don't you try weighing some fruits or vegetables such as a banana or 2 apples. You could also see if you can guess how much you think something will weigh and then put it on the scales to see what the result is.

SHARING & DIVIDING

When you have made a large quantity of mixture, you may need to divide it up into small amounts before you cook it. For example, for the burgers on page 64, you need to divide the mixture into 8 equal pieces. To do this, first cut the mixture into 2 equal pieces (halves), then cut each half in half to make 4 equal pieces (quarters) and then cut each quarter in half again to make eighths.

SHAPING

Use your hands to help you shape any mixture.

RUBBING BUTTER INTO FLOUR

Once you know how to rub fat into flour you can make pastry, crumble toppings, or cookies. Make sure that the butter is really cold. Use a table knife to cut the cold butter into small pieces, add to the flour, and gently rub the pieces of butter between the tips of your thumbs and fingers so they flatten and gradually mix into the flour. Keep lifting your fingertips above the bowl, as this will let air get to the flour and keep the mixture cool. Try not to use your whole hands, as this will melt the butter.

CREAMING BUTTER & SUGAR

The most common way to make cakes and many cookies is to begin by creaming together softened butter with sugar—this means beating the sugar and butter together either with a wooden spoon or an electric mixer until the mixture is very pale and fluffy. This adds air to the mixture and gives it a light and fluffy, almost mousselike texture. Before you begin: use unsalted butter (it has a better flavor than margarine) and you will need to take it out of the fridge some time before you start so that it is soft. If the butter is too hard you will not be able to beat in a lot of air and the cake may not rise as well.

FOLDING

This is when you carefully mix a cake mixture, almost cutting it with the spoon to "fold" it rather than mix it. This method adds air to the mixture so that it stays light and airy. It is easier if you use a metal spoon instead of a wooden spoon.

BREADCRUMBING

Dip the food into a little beaten egg, then dip into bread crumbs and turn to coat the food evenly.

MARINATING

A marinade can actually start to soften food and break it down, so do you need to be careful how long you let the food sit in marinade. For example, fish left to marinate in lemon juice and oil will start to cook as it sits in the lemon juice.

HOW TO CRACK AN EGG

There are 2 ways to crack eggs. Either hold an egg in one hand and carefully use a table knife to crack the egg in the middle. Put your thumbs into the crack and pull the egg shell apart. Let the egg fall into a pitcher or bowl and mix with a fork. Fish out any egg shell with a spoon. Or, if you prefer, you can crack an egg by bashing it on the side of a bowl, but you might end up with some of the egg dripping down the side of the bowl until you've had a chance to practice! Always wash your hands well after cracking eggs, as it is very easy to pass bacteria from raw food like eggs to cooked food.

OPENING CANS

This will take some practice and you need to be careful, as cans are sharp. Ask an adult to show you how to use your can opener, as they all differ.

MELTING CHOCOLATE & BUTTER

Heat the chocolate and butter very, very gently in a saucepan over low heat so that the chocolate melts slowly.

KITCHEN EQUIPMENT

There's lots more to explore in the kitchen now that you are getting used to cooking and using different types of equipment. Here are a few that might be good to try.

MEASURING CUPS

You will need a glass measuring cup for liquids and a set of measuring cups for dry ingredients.

SAUCEPANS

Ideally you need a small saucepan for pasta sauces and a large pan for cooking pasta (see page 94).

SMALL, SHARP KNIFE

A small paring knife is the best knife to begin with. Once you know how to hold your knife and cut food safely, there are so many things that you can make to eat. The two main cutting techniques are the "bridge" and the "claw" techniques (see page 50, above). Once you have learned how to master these, you can cut most things safely, but always ask an adult before you use a sharp knife.

SPATULA

This is ideal for scraping a bowl clean, but you might prefer to use your fingers (if the mixture is safe to eat—check with an adult)!

CAN OPENER

Some foods come in cans and some cans have a ring pull, which makes them easy to open. Others will require a can opener. Let an adult help you the first time you use one.

LEMON JUICER

If you don't have a juicer, cut the fruit into smaller pieces and squeeze the juice out by hand. You will probably need to strain the juice to ensure that you remove any seeds.

BAKING PANS

Loaf pans, small round pans, or square pans are all used to bake cakes.

ROUND CUTTER

This is helpful for cutting out cookies or small tarts like on page 56 but if you don't have a cutter, you can use a small cup or bowl instead. Cutters can come in other shapes, too, for making cookies.

OVENPROOF DISH

You will need a dish that won't crack when you put it into the oven for recipes like the what's-in-season fruit crumble on page 76. These come in different shapes, sizes, and colors and you will probably have a couple in your kitchen cupboard.

SCALES

The great thing with cooking is that you can practice things you are learning at school, like maths, when you measure and weigh out ingredients. Ask your parents if they have a scale that you can use. There are lots of different types, so ask an adult to show you how to use them.

GARLIC PRESS

This is easy and good fun to use. Make sure that you peel the pink skin away from the garlic clove before you crush it.

GRATER

Remember that the small "teeth" can be as sharp as little knives, so make sure that you always keep your fingers away from them. Graters come in different shapes and sizes and the "teeth" on the graters vary in size.

PALETTE KNIFE

This is handy for lifting things.

herby scrambled eggs

Did you know that the yolk of the egg is orange and the clear part is called the white? Scrambled eggs are a great, simple recipe to learn, as once you know how to make them, you can make them for your lunch, breakfast, or supper.

For 1 person you need:

INGREDIENTS
fresh herb e.g. parsley leaves or chives
2 free-range eggs
4 cherry tomatoes
a little unsalted butter
buttered toast, to eat with the eggs

EQUIPMENT
scissors ◆ mixing bowl ◆ table knife
spoon ◆ fork ◆ small paring knife
saucepan ◆ heatproof trivet

1 Using scissors, snip some herbs into small pieces and put in a mixing bowl. Now you need to crack open the eggs: hold an egg in one hand and carefully use a table knife to crack the egg in the middle. Put your thumbs into the crack and pull the egg shell apart. Let the egg fall into the bowl. Repeat with the other egg. Fish out any egg shell with a spoon. (See page 60 for a photo of how to crack eggs.) Mix with a fork.

2 Use the bridge-cutting technique to cut the tomatoes: make a "bridge" with a thumb and finger of one hand and hold the tomato. Hold a small paring knife in your other hand and put the blade under the bridge, then cut downward firmly. Now cut each half into quarters and add to the eggs.

3 Put the butter in a saucepan. Melt over medium (not high) heat. Add the eggs and cook, stirring with a spoon. Keep stirring to break up the egg.

4 When the eggs are almost cooked—so they look only slightly wet—take the pan off the heat and rest on a heatproof trivet. Keep stirring until the eggs are cooked—the heat from the pan will continue to cook them. Eat with toast.

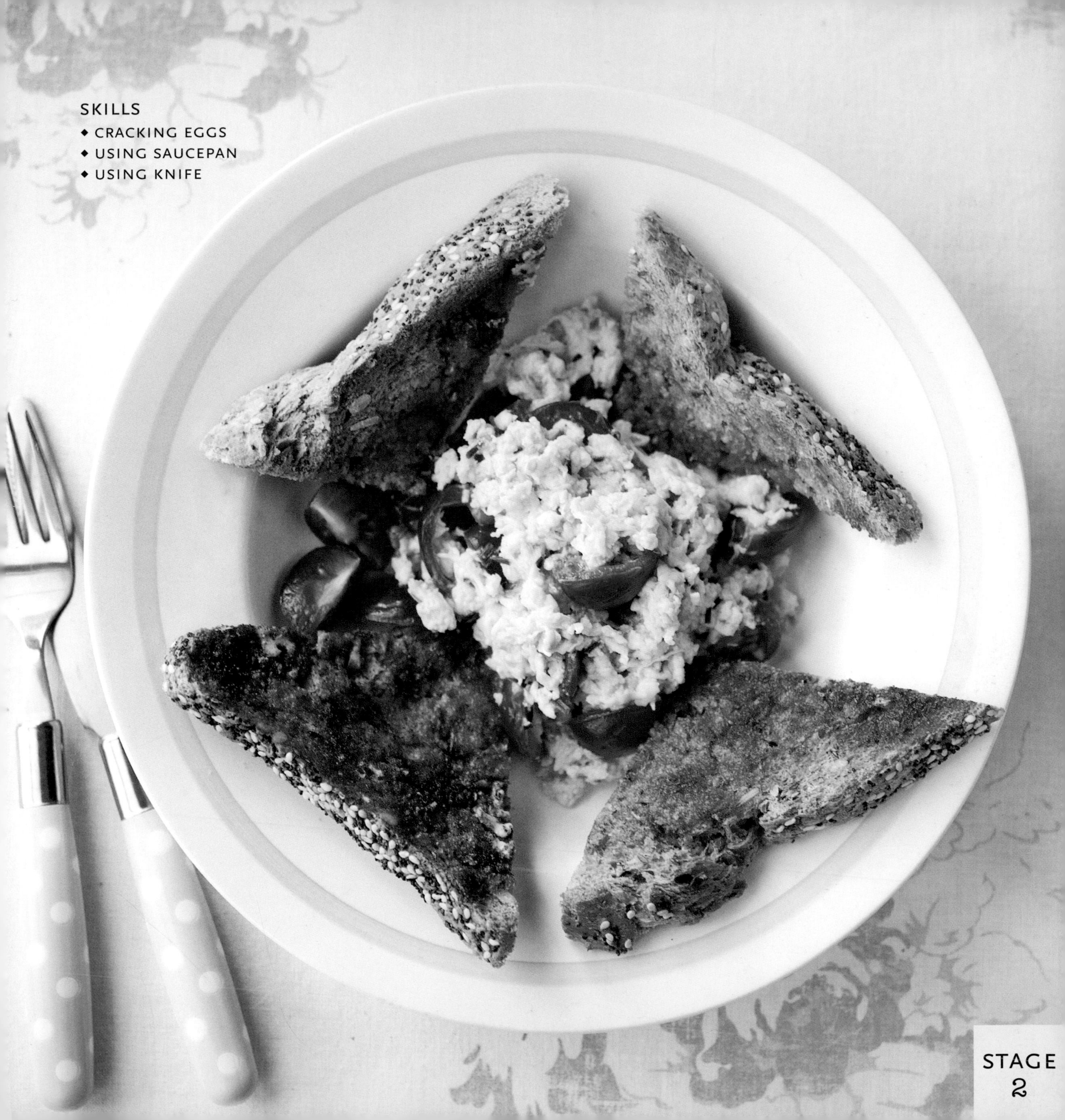
SKILLS
◆ CRACKING EGGS
◆ USING SAUCEPAN
◆ USING KNIFE
STAGE
2

mini puffy tomato tarts

Thanks to Libby and Tess for testing this recipe. They found it great fun rolling out the dough, cutting out circles, and spreading the pesto on top. If you haven't used a grater before, make sure you keep your fingers away from the sharp "teeth."

SKILLS
- ROLLING PASTRY
- CUTTING CIRCLES
- SPREADING
- CHOOSING TOPPINGS
- USING OVEN

To make 10 mini tarts you need:

INGREDIENTS
3 big handfuls ripe cherry tomatoes
about 1 oz. cheddar cheese
6½ oz. puff pastry dough
a little flour for sprinkling
4–5 teaspoons pesto (or sun-dried tomato paste)
you could also try other toppings like chopped olives, chorizo, or salami

EQUIPMENT
cutting board ◆ small paring knife grater ◆ rolling pin ◆ 2 pennies ◆ round cutter about 2½ inches across ◆ 2 nonstick baking sheets ◆ spoon ◆ oven mitts

1 Use the bridge-cutting technique to cut the tomatoes: on a cutting board, make a "bridge" with a thumb and finger of one hand and hold the tomato. Hold a small paring knife in your other hand and put the blade under the bridge, then cut downward firmly. Now cut each half into quarters.

2 To grate the cheese, hold the handle of the grater with one hand and use the other hand to push the cheese downward over the grater "teeth." Always keep your fingers away from the grater "teeth" as they are very sharp.

3 Break the dough in half. Sprinkle a little flour on the work surface. Roll one piece of dough with a rolling pin until it is about the same thickness as 2 stacked pennies.

4 Take the round cutter and, starting at the edge of the dough, push it down into the dough to cut out circles. Keep going until you have used up all of that dough. Roll out the other piece of dough and make more circles.

5 Put the circles of dough on the baking sheets. Use a teaspoon to spread a bit of pesto over each circle. Try to leave a little border around the edge of the circles of dough—this will help the dough to puff up around the pesto when it cooks.

6 Put a few pieces of tomato on top of the pesto and, if you like olives, chorizo, or salami, chop some and add those too. Sprinkle the grated cheese over the tarts. Ask an adult to help you put the baking sheets into the oven using oven mitts. Cook for 15 minutes. The dough should be cooked and slightly puffy and the cheese will have melted.

STAGE
2

pretty shrimp cocktails

This is a great lunch, or if you want to have a special meal you could make this for an appetizer instead of having dessert. Did you know that shrimp are gray when they are raw and they turn pink when they are cooked?

For 4 people you need:

INGREDIENTS
4 tablespoons mayonnaise
2 tablespoons tomato ketchup
¼ lemon
about 10 crisp lettuce leaves
8 oz. cooked, peeled shrimp
a little paprika

EQUIPMENT
spoon • small bowl • colander • clean kitchen towel • 4 small plates or bowls

1 Count the spoons of mayonnaise and ketchup into a small bowl.
2 Squeeze the juice from the lemon quarter into the bowl and mix everything together with the spoon to make a pink sauce.
3 Put the lettuce in a colander and wash in the sink. Gently shake the lettuce to dry it or spread it on a clean kitchen towel to dry out. Tear the lettuce into big chunks.
4 Share the chunks of lettuce between 4 small plates or bowls, then share the shrimp out evenly too, and put them on top of the lettuce. Spoon a little pink sauce on top of each. Take a small pinch of paprika with your fingers and sprinkle over each shrimp cocktail.

SKILLS
◆ COUNTING
◆ SQUEEZING LEMONS
◆ WASHING VEGETABLES
◆ DIVIDING

pink fish sandwich

You can make these whenever you have some spare time in the day and then keep them in the fridge until you are ready to cook them. Instead of adding lemon zest to the bread crumb mixture you could try lime, or to make green fish fingers add lots of fresh chopped herbs to the bread crumbs. All three of my children insisted that this recipe went in the book, as they love making them with their friends!

For 4 people you need:

INGREDIENTS
8 thin salmon fillets (or white fish like haddock), cut into strips by an adult
2 free-range eggs
about 8 tablespoons bread crumbs
1 unwaxed lemon or lime or handful fresh herbs
8 tablespoons all-purpose flour
8 thick slices bread, some sliced tomatoes, and watercress or lettuce

EQUIPMENT
scissors • parchment paper
2 baking sheets • table knife
3 small bowls • spoon • fork
small grater • oven mitts

1 Turn the oven on to 375°F. Cut 2 pieces of parchment paper, each big enough to cover the baking sheets. Rub your finger all over the fish to check for bones. If you feel a sharp bone sticking out, pull it out with your fingers.

2 To crack open the eggs, hold an egg in one hand and carefully use a table knife to crack the egg in the middle. Put your thumbs into the crack and pull the egg shell apart. Let the egg fall into a small bowl. Repeat with the other egg. Fish out any egg shell with a spoon. Mix with a fork.

3 Put the bread crumbs into a small bowl. To grate the lemon or lime, hold the handle of the grater with one hand and use the other hand to push the fruit downward over the grater "teeth." Always keep your fingers away from the grater "teeth," as they are very sharp. Add the zest to the bread crumbs.

4 Count the spoons of flour into a small bowl. Dip the fish first into the flour, then the beaten egg, then the bread crumbs so that the fish is well coated. Put the fish pieces on the baking sheets.

4

Ask an adult to help you put the sheets into the oven using oven mitts. Bake for 10–15 minutes or until the fish is golden and cooked all the way through —ask an adult to help you check this. Ask an adult to help you take the sheets out of the oven using oven mitts. Put the fish pieces inside some bread with sliced tomatoes and watercress.

SKILLS
♦ BREADCRUMBING
♦ CRACKING EGGS
♦ USING OVEN
♦ ZESTING LEMON

minty lamb couscous

This is great to make after you have had roast lamb for a Sunday dinner. However, if you haven't had a roast, you could try adding other ingredients instead like canned fish, crumbled feta cheese, chopped tomatoes, fresh herbs, chopped cucumber, watercress, grated carrot etc. and then mix with Susan's salad dressing from page 18 instead of the mint jelly.

For 4 people you need:

INGREDIENTS

1⅓ cups couscous
1 cup boiling water (or just enough to cover the couscous)
2 large handfuls dried apricots
1 large zucchini or 2 small zucchini
about 3 teaspoons mint jelly
a few handfuls leftover roast lamb, chopped
freshly ground black pepper, if you like

EQUIPMENT

heatproof bowl ◆ measuring cups ◆ fork ◆ scissors ◆ grater

1 Weigh the couscous. How you weigh it will depend on the weighing scales that you use. (See pages 50 and 52 for more information about how to weigh ingredients.) Put the couscous into a heatproof bowl.
2 Ask an adult or older child to boil some water and pour the boiling water into a measuring cup up to the 1-cup mark. Pour this water carefully over the couscous. Leave the couscous for about 5 minutes and watch as the hard grains absorb the hot water and become soft and fluffy.
3 Use a fork or your hands to mix the couscous and break up the grains. The grains will feel lovely and soft!

4 Using scissors, snip the apricots into small pieces. To grate the zucchini, hold the handle of the grater with one hand and use the other hand to push the zucchini downward over the grater "teeth." Always keep your fingers away from the grater "teeth," as they are very sharp. Add the zucchini and apricots to the couscous. Add the mint jelly and chopped roast lamb to the couscous and mix everything together. Taste the mixture and add a little black pepper if you think it needs it.

SKILLS ◆ PREPARING COUSCOUS ◆ MEASURING LIQUID
USING SCISSORS ◆ GRATING

4

oven-baked herby burgers

Lots of children have helped to test the recipes in this book, especially Rosie, Libby, and Tess. They all felt that the book should have a burger recipe in it and they found this oven-baked burger recipe easy to cook and good to eat.

1 Turn the oven on to 375°F. Dip a pastry brush into a little olive or vegetable oil and brush it all over a baking sheet. This will stop the burgers from sticking to the sheet.

2 Using a table knife, cut the cheese into small pieces on a cutting board.

3 Using scissors, snip the herb into small pieces and put into a mixing bowl. Still using scissors, snip the ends off the scallions and throw away, then snip the scallions into tiny pieces and put in the bowl.

4 Now you need to crack open the egg: hold it in one hand and carefully use a table knife to crack the egg in the middle. Put your thumbs into the crack and pull the egg shell apart. Let the egg fall into a small bowl. Fish out any egg shell with a spoon. (See page 60 for a photo of how to crack eggs.) Mix with a fork.

5 Put the ground beef, chopped cheese, and egg into the bowl with the herbs and scallions and mix everything together really well with your hands.

6 Break the beef mixture in half and then break each piece in half again to make 4 pieces (quarters). Now break each quarter in half again to make 8 pieces (eighths). Roll each piece into a ball with your hands, then put onto the oiled baking sheet and flatten into a burger shape. Do the same with all

To make 8 small burgers you need:

INGREDIENTS

a little olive or vegetable oil
about 1 oz. cheddar cheese
small handful fresh herbs e.g. parsley,
cilantro, or thyme
2 scallions
1 free-range egg
1 lb. good-quality ground beef round or
sirloin (don't buy extra-lean otherwise
your burger will be too dry)
8 small burger buns, some lettuce, sliced
tomatoes, and tomato ketchup

EQUIPMENT

pastry brush ◆ baking sheet ◆ table knife
cutting board ◆ scissors ◆ mixing bowl
small bowl ◆ spoon ◆ fork ◆ palette knife
oven mitts

the pieces. Now, WASH YOUR HANDS
—you must always wash your hands
thoroughly after handling raw meat. Ask an
adult to help you put the sheet into the oven
using oven mitts. Cook for 8 minutes. Ask
an adult to help you take the sheet out of
the oven using oven mitts. Using a palette
knife, turn the burgers over and put back in
the oven for 8 more minutes or until cooked
in the middle. Eat in buns with lettuce,
tomatoes, and ketchup.

Tip: To make lamb burgers, swap the beef
for lamb and add thyme leaves, plus snipped
dried apricots instead of cheddar cheese.

SKILLS

◆ CHOPPING WITH TABLE KNIFE
◆ USING SCISSORS
◆ CRACKING EGGS
◆ COUNTING
◆ DIVIDING
◆ SHAPING
◆ USING OVEN

STAGE
2

broiled ham bagel

Help your parents out by making your own snack or lunch. Just remember that the broiler is hot and you must have an adult with you when you use it. Choose a favorite chutney to spread over the top. If your bagel is for lunch, try to have some chopped cucumber, celery, or carrot with it. It is a good idea to have a vegetable or fruit with every meal and snack, so that you eat your "5 a day."

To make 1 bagel you need:

INGREDIENTS
1 bagel, cut in half
1 slice ham
small piece cheddar cheese
chutney, if you like

EQUIPMENT
baking sheet ◆ grater ◆ oven mitts
table knife

SKILLS
◆ USING BROILER
◆ GRATING
◆ SPREADING

1 Turn the broiler on—you will need to ask an adult to show you how to do this, as all broilers are different. Put the bagel halves, cut-side up, onto a baking sheet. Tear the ham and put onto the bagel halves around the holes in the middle. Avoid the hole otherwise the ham will fall into it!

2 To grate the cheese, hold the handle of the grater with one hand and use the other hand to push the cheese downward over the grater "teeth." Always keep your fingers away from the grater "teeth," as they are very sharp. Sprinkle the cheese on the ham.

3 Ask an adult to help you put the baking sheet under the broiler using oven mitts. Broil for 3–4 minutes or until the cheese is golden and bubbling. Keep watching it—this will only take a few minutes and if you leave it under the broiler for too long it might burn. Ask an adult to help you take the sheet from under the broiler using oven mitts and see how the cheese has melted!

4 Spread a little chutney over the top.

tropical smoothie

Papayas have a green skin that turns yellow as it ripens and the orange flesh is sweet. Passion fruits are small and dark, and their skin wrinkles when it ripens. The skin can be quite tough, so you may need to ask for help with cutting through it. Most smoothies are made using a blender, but they have a very sharp blade that cuts the fruit into tiny pieces, so ask an adult to help you when you use one.

To make 2 glasses you need:

INGREDIENTS
1 ripe papaya (about 1 lb.)
1 passion fruit
1 ripe banana
2 small glasses fresh orange juice

EQUIPMENT
cutting board ♦ small paring knife
spoon ♦ blender ♦ spoon ♦ 2 tall glasses

SKILLS
♦ USING BLENDER
♦ CHOPPING WITH PARING KNIFE

1 Use the bridge-cutting technique to cut the pawpaw in half lengthwise: on a cutting board, make a "bridge" with a thumb and finger of one hand and hold the papaya. Hold a small paring knife in your other hand and put the blade under the bridge, then cut downward firmly. Cut the passion fruit in half in the same way. You might ask an adult or older child to help you, as passion fruits are quite tough. Using a spoon, scrape the black seeds out of the papaya and throw away.

2 Peel the banana, break it into 2 or 3 pieces and put into the blender. Using a teaspoon, scoop the orange papaya flesh into the blender, too. Now scrape the seeds and juice from the passion fruit on top of the papaya.

3 Pour the orange juice in the blender, put the lid on, and blend until smooth. (Ask an adult or older child to help you.)

4 Pour the smoothie into 2 tall glasses.

STAGE
2

Finley's lemonberryade

Finley likes to make this when we have friends over. The lemonade without the raspberries will keep for at least a week in a bottle in the fridge. If you do add raspberries, only add them when you are ready to drink the lemonade.

1 You might like to ask an adult to help you with this, as lemons are quite tough to cut. Use the bridge-cutting technique to cut the lemons: on a cutting board, make a "bridge" with a thumb and finger of one hand and hold the lemon. Hold a small paring knife in your other hand and put the blade under the bridge, then cut downward firmly.

2 Put a lemon half over a lemon juicer and press down. Try to turn the lemon as you press down. If you don't have a lemon juicer, you might like to try cutting the lemon half in half again using the bridge-cutting technique to make quarters and then squeeze the lemon quarters with your hands.

3 Before you pour the juice into a nice pitcher, if there are any seeds in the juice, pour it through a strainer into the pitcher to catch the seeds.

4 Add the sugar to the pitcher and stir with a big spoon until the sugar has dissolved (or disappeared).

5 Use a measuring cup to measure 4 cups cold water and add to the lemon juice in the pitcher.

6 When you are ready to drink the lemonberryade, put the raspberries in a bowl and mash with a fork. Add them to the lemonade and stir. You need to strain the lemonade again into another pitcher, pushing the raspberries though the strainer with a fork as you go.

5

6

To make 8 glasses you need:

INGREDIENTS
4 lemons
⅔ cup natural cane sugar
4 cups cold water
handful fresh raspberries
ice cubes, if you want to make
the drink cold!

EQUIPMENT
cutting board ◆ small paring knife
lemon juicer ◆ small strainer
nice pitcher ◆ big spoon ◆ fork
measuring cups ◆ small bowl

Tips: If you are going to drink this lemonade as soon as you have made it, you could try using sparkling water to make it fizzy!

And now that you know how to juice fruit, you might like to make some freshly squeezed orange juice for breakfast.

STAGE
2

flower & herb ice bowl

I first made one of these in my home economics (now called design technology) lessons at school and I still remember how cool I thought it was to have made my own bowl. You could scoop your favorite ice cream or sorbet into the middle, or just put fresh summer fruits inside. Whatever you choose, I bet your friends will be impressed with the bowl. Remember, you will need to be patient and wait several hours until this is frozen.

To make 1 beautiful ice bowl you need:

INGREDIENTS
fresh edible flowers and/or fresh herbs or any pretty leaves from the garden (we used pink rose petals, rosemary, thyme, and sage)

You might like to fill your bowl with a yogurt and fruit mix like the berry crunch on page 40, but you will need to make more to fill your ice bowl (without the cereal). You will also need lots of fresh raspberries and strawberries.

EQUIPMENT
big freezerproof bowl • small freezerproof bowl • small weight • sticky tape • clean kitchen towel • plate

1 Take your 2 bowls and pour enough cold water into the big bowl to half fill it. Scatter some fresh flowers and/or herbs in the water.

2 Rest the small bowl inside the big bowl and put a small weight in the small bowl to help it sit still. Stretch sticky tape across the tops of the bowls in several directions to hold the small bowl in place inside the big bowl. Put in the freezer and leave overnight.

3 The next day, peel off the sticky tape and carefully pull the small bowl out of the big bowl.

4 Lay a clean kitchen towel on the work surface and tip the big bowl upside down to let the ice bowl slip out. Turn the ice bowl the right way up and sit it on a plate. Fill your ice bowl with the yogurt and fruit mix and top with fresh raspberries and strawberries.

Tip: You might need to sit the big bowl in a little warm water to help ease the ice bowl out of it, but don't leave it sitting in warm water for long otherwise it will melt.

SKILLS
◆ FREEZING
◆ PICKING FRESH HERBS

shortbread shapes

If ever my children want to bake and we don't seem to have much in the cupboard, this is what they make. When you choose your cutters for making the shortbread shapes, make sure they are roughly the same size, because if you put big shortbreads onto a baking sheet with little shortbreads, the little shortbreads will be cooked a long time before the big ones! This recipe makes a lot of shapes—the number will depend on the size of the cutters that you choose.

To make lots of shortbread shapes you need:

INGREDIENTS
1 stick unsalted butter, soft
¼ cup natural cane sugar plus a little extra
1 capful vanilla extract
1⅓ cups all-purpose flour
1 tablespoon milk

EQUIPMENT
scissors • parchment paper

baking sheet • mixing bowl
wooden spoon • rolling pin
2 pennies • shaped cutters
fork • oven mitts

SKILLS
• LINING SHEETS
• CREAMING
• ROLLING
• CUTTING
• USING OVEN

1 Turn the oven on to 375°F. Cut a piece of parchment paper big enough to cover the baking sheet.
2 Put the soft butter, sugar, and vanilla extract in a mixing bowl and mix well with a wooden spoon until it becomes fluffy and paler in color. This helps to beat air into the mixture.
3 Add the flour and milk to the bowl and mix until the mixture comes together to form a ball. You can do this with your hands or the wooden spoon.
4 Break the dough into 3 pieces. Sprinkle a little flour over the work surface and the rolling pin. Flatten one piece of dough

with a rolling pin until it is the same thickness as 2 stacked pennies. Take the cutters you have chosen and, starting at the edge of the dough, push them down into the dough to cut out shapes. Repeat with the rest of the dough pieces.
5 Carefully lift the shapes onto the baking sheet, then press a fork gently onto the shortbread to make pretty patterns. Sprinkle a little sugar over the top of the shortbread. Ask an adult to help you put the sheet in the oven using oven mitts. Bake for 10 minutes (if they are small shapes) or 15 minutes (if they are big shapes), or until golden.

what's-in-season fruit crumble

One of the first things my mom taught me to make was a crumble. It's a great way to learn how to rub butter into flour. Once you know how to do this you can have a go at making pastry (see page 114). You can sprinkle this crumble mix on top of so many different fruits. Try to choose fruit that is in season—if you are not sure what that is, ask the person working in the produce section of your supermarket or go to a local farmers market. Berries are easy to use as you don't need to chop them first.

1 Turn the oven on to 350°F. To make the fruit filling, use the bridge-cutting technique to cut the plums in half: on a cutting board, make a "bridge" with a thumb and finger of one hand and hold the plum. Hold a small paring knife in your other hand and put the blade under the bridge, then cut downward firmly. Move the plums around as you cut to avoid cutting through the pit. Take out the pits.
2 Put the plums into 2 small or 1 large ovenproof dish. Pour the orange juice over the plums, add the sugar and flour, and mix with a spoon or your hands.

3 To make the crumble topping, put the flour into a bowl, add the butter, and rub the butter into the flour with your fingers until it looks like fine bread crumbs (see page 114 for photos showing you how to do this). This can take a few minutes. Add the oats, sugar, and spice and mix with your fingers again.
4 Spoon the mixture over the top of the plums. Ask an adult to help you put the dishes into the oven using oven mitts. Bake for 25–30 minutes, or until the crumble topping is crisp, the plums are soft, and the fruit juices are bubbling up around the edges.

4

SKILLS
- RUBBING IN
- CUTTING WITH KNIFE
- MIXING WITH SPOON
- SPRINKLING TOPPING

For 4–6 people you need:

FRUIT FILLING

seasonal fruit e.g. 15 plums or about
1 lb. 4 oz. fresh or frozen berries or
about 12 peaches or nectarines
4 tablespoons orange juice
3 tablespoons light brown sugar
1 tablespoon all-purpose flour

CRUMBLE TOPPING

1 cup plus 2 tablespoons all-purpose
flour
6½ tablespoons unsalted butter, chilled
and cut into small pieces
2 handfuls oats (or muesli if you prefer)
4 tablespoons light brown sugar
1 teaspoon apple pie spice or ground
cinnamon

EQUIPMENT

cutting board ◆ *small paring knife*
spoon ◆ *2 small or 1 large ovenproof dish*

STAGE
2

Ella's marshmallow & chocolate squares

Ella made this recipe up one day when she found some chocolate and marshmallows in the cupboard. She asked me how much butter and syrup to add and then she did the rest! This is only to be eaten occasionally, as it is very, very sweet! Remember, you will need to be patient while you wait for it to set.

To make about 30 small pieces you need:

INGREDIENTS
12 graham crackers or digestive biscuits
¾ cup mini-marshmallows
1 cup dried fruit e.g. raisins, chopped mango, chopped apricots
3½ oz. milk chocolate
6½ oz. unsalted butter, chopped into big chunks
5 tablespoons golden syrup

EQUIPMENT
mixing bowl • large saucepan teaspoon • wooden spoon parchment paper • any cake pan (round, square or loaf pan) • scissors • table knife

SKILLS
◆ MELTING CHOCOLATE
◆ MIXING
◆ SETTING IN FRIDGE

1 Using a scrap of parchment paper, rub a little butter inside the cake pan. Now using scissors, cut a piece of parchment to fit along the bottom of the pan and up the ends. Fit it inside the pan. Put the graham crackers into a mixing bowl. Break them into small pieces. Add the mini-marshmallows and dried fruit.

2 Break the chocolate into small pieces and put into a large saucepan with the butter. Add the golden syrup—you might need to use a teaspoon to scrape the syrup off the tablespoon.

3 Ask an adult to help you turn the burner onto low heat and put the pan over it. Leave for a few minutes until the chocolate starts to melt. Stir everything with a wooden spoon until it's smooth. Take the pan off the heat, add the fruit mixture, and stir everything together.

4 Spoon the mixture into the pan and push it down with the spoon. Cover with parchment paper and put in the fridge for 4 hours or until hard. Pull the ends of the parchment paper up at each end of the pan and pull the mixture out—you may need to run a table knife along the sides to help release it from the pan. Cut into small pieces and put into a jar.

4

STAGE 3
7-11 YEARS

Grownups: this page is for you

CHILDREN: YOU CAN SKIP THIS BIT AND HAVE FUN COOKING!

This age range is huge. Some children will be able to cook independently and others will still need some assistance. But here are a few things that your child will be beginning to do during this stage. Remind your child that she can go back to Stage 1 of the book as she will find those recipes easy to make.

♦ It is likely that your child will be well into the swing of following the recipes on her own by now, and will be gaining independence and confidence in the kitchen. This is what this book is all about!

♦ She will enjoy the chance to try new pieces of kitchen equipment. Try to stand back and let her feel that she is in control, at the same time being nearby if help is needed. It is very easy to take over in the kitchen, so try to hold back.

♦ By now, most children like to cook with a friend or sibling. The sooner children realize that cooking is a fun and sociable activity, the better!

♦ She will have an increased ability to remember and should be able to easily repeat skills from the previous chapters. These new skills will be with her now for life.

♦ Her coordination will be greatly improved and she will have more control over smaller muscles, making it easier to complete more intricate tasks.

♦ She will be able to plan ahead more easily, for example if she is helping to make a meal, she will have a better understanding of timing and planning.

♦ She is likely to be keen to understand more about the science behind food, for example about yeast and kneading, and about cake making.

♦ Children at this age still enjoy learning through play, which is one reason why cooking is so great, as she can learn essential life skills while having fun in the kitchen.

♦ She will be able to start to teach other family members her new-found skills.

♦ Some children will be ready to cook a two- or even three-course meal for the family using the recipes from all the stages in this book— enjoy being cooked for!

♦ Make sure she helps to clear up after she has finished cooking! This is a really important life skill.

KITCHEN EQUIPMENT

You have already used most of the basic kitchen utensils, but there are just a few other utensils that are worth mentioning in case you choose to cook all the recipes in this chapter.

TRIVET

As it sounds, this is a small heatproof stand for resting hot pans on. It is very handy to have a trivet by the stovetop. You can then take something out of the oven or off the stove and put it on the trivet. Never put anything hot onto the kitchen work surface, as you might damage the surface.

PASTA PAN

A pasta pan has its own colander inside the pan, ready for draining the pasta when it is cooked. Most Italians have a pasta pan, as they like to cook pasta a lot. It doesn't matter if you don't have one—just use a large pan and a colander instead. (Always ask an adult to drain the pasta for you, as the pan will be heavy and full of boiling water.)

ROASTING DISH

Ideally you need a heavy-based roasting dish. This will heat up and cook the food without burning it.

WOK OR LARGE FRYING PAN

Now that you are used to cooking on the stovetop, you might like to try making the stir-fry on page 92. The best pan for a stir-fry is a wok, as it is large enough to give you space to toss the vegetables around and "stir" them as you "fry." If you don't have a wok, you could use a large frying pan.

FLUTED CUTTERS

Some cook stores sell these individually, or you could buy a set so that you have different-sized cutters to play with.

12-HOLE CUPCAKE PAN

This pan is ideal for making small cakes or tarts. Once you know how to make pastry, you can make up your own tart recipe.

2 x 8-INCH CAKE PANS

If you only have one cake pan and you want to make a layer cake like a Victoria sponge cake where you sandwich 2 cakes together, you need to make half the batter and bake it, then make the other half and bake it. Or you can see if a neighbor or friend has another cake pan you could use.

SUSHI MAT OR NAPKIN

You don't have to have a sushi mat to make sushi—you can use a napkin instead. A sushi mat is used to help roll the sushi into a long sausage shape.

BOWLS FOR MARINATING

When you marinate fish, meat, or vegetables, put the marinade ingredients in a glass, Pyrex, melamine, or plastic bowl, not a metal one. Acidic ingredients like lemon juice and vinegar can react with the metal and give the food a funny taste.

WHISKS

You will need either a balloon whisk or an electric mixer to whisk egg whites until they are white and fluffy. I always recommend that if possible you have a go at whisking with a balloon whisk to practice how to whisk. You can always use an electric mixer later to see the difference.

SMALL PUDDING BASINS

These are good to have for making small baked desserts or you could use them for setting jellies. You might also hear an adult suggest that you use ramekins. These are small dishes that can be put into the oven.

VEGETABLE PEELER

These can be quite tricky to use, so you may need to have a go with friends' peelers until you find one that you are happy with.

SMALL GRATER

Some big graters have small holes on them that you can use for grating ingredients that you want to make tiny pieces from. If your big grater doesn't have small enough holes, you will need a small grater.

ham & pineapple pizzas

We often have these on a Saturday night. They are fun to make and cheaper than going out for pizza in a restaurant. Did you know that yeast is alive? It is a living micro-organism used to make bread rise and give it a lighter, more open texture. For the yeast to work, it needs to grow (or reproduce). To do this it needs warmth (from warm water), moisture (water), and food (sugar from the flour). The yeast produces a gas, carbon dioxide, which makes the bread rise before it is baked. We bake pizzas in a very hot oven to kill the yeast so that they don't carry on rising.

1 Put the flour into a mixing bowl. Sprinkle the yeast over the top.

2 Make a well (a hole) in the middle of the flour with your hand. Pour the warm water into a measuring cup until it is just below the 1-cup mark. Make sure the water is warm and not too hot—when you put your finger in, it should feel just warm. Add the olive oil to the water, then pour into the well. Use a wooden spoon to stir the liquid, and the flour will gradually fall into the water. Keep stirring until all the flour is mixed with the liquid and you have a dough.

3 Sprinkle a little flour over the work surface, take the dough out of the bowl, and knead it. The best way to knead is to push the dough down and away with the heel of the hand and then pull it back with your fingers. Push it back onto the work surface, turn the dough slightly and then repeat. After a few minutes of doing this, the dough should have a smooth, elastic texture.

4 Clean the mixing bowl and put the dough back in. Now cover it with plastic wrap or a clean kitchen towel and leave it somewhere warm to rise for about an hour, or until it is twice as big—look how much the dough has grown!

5 Turn the oven on to 400°F. Dip a pastry brush into a little olive oil and brush it all over the baking sheets. Break the risen dough in half and, using a rolling pin, roll each piece into two large flat circles.

6 Lift the pizza crusts onto the baking sheets. Spread the tomato purée over the crusts with the back of a spoon.

To make 2 very large or 3–4 small pizzas you need:

PIZZA DOUGH
2¾ cups all-purpose flour
7-g packet instant yeast
2 tablespoons olive oil plus a little extra
1 scant cup warm (not hot) water

TOPPINGS
tomato purée, ham, pineapple, mozzarella, and grated cheese OR tomato purée, shrimp, and sliced bell peppers OR any other topping combinations that you might like to try

EQUIPMENT
mixing bowl ◆ measuring cup ◆ wooden spoon ◆ plastic wrap ◆ pastry brush 2 baking sheets ◆ rolling pin ◆ spoon oven mitts

Did you know? Kneading the dough helps to distribute the yeast cells evenly and give the dough elasticity (which means it is stretchy). You may need to knead for up to 10 minutes before the dough is smooth, elastic, and almost silky to touch. To test if the dough has been kneaded for long enough, roll it into a ball and prod it with your finger—it should spring back quickly.

SKILLS
◆ MAKING YEAST DOUGH
◆ ROLLING
◆ SPREADING
◆ USING OVEN

7 Scatter your ham and pineapple over the tomato. Using oven mitts, put the sheets in the oven and bake for 15–20 minutes or until the crusts are cooked.

tacos with soybeans & cilantro

The mild chili powder in this recipe gives the beans a slight chili flavor, but you can always leave it out if you really don't like it—they will still taste good. This simple meal is as fun to make as it is to eat because there are lots of things to assemble, and so lots of things to try!

For 4 people you need:

INGREDIENTS

14 oz. canned chopped tomatoes
2 x 14-oz. cans soybeans in water
(or pinto beans)
2 scallions
1 garlic clove
1 tablespoon olive oil
1 teaspoon ground coriander
1 teaspoon mild chili powder
1 teaspoon sugar
handful cilantro leaves plus a
little extra
8–12 tacos
2 ripe avocados
⅔ cup sour cream
grated cheddar cheese
pieces of lime

EQUIPMENT

*can opener ◆ colander ◆ small paring
knife ◆ cutting board ◆ garlic press
small saucepan ◆ wooden spoon
baking sheet ◆ oven mitts ◆ spoon*

SKILLS

**OPENING CANS ◆ CUTTING
CRUSHING GARLIC ◆ USING
STOVETOP ◆ USING OVEN**

1 Turn the oven on to 350°F. Use a can opener to open the cans of tomatoes and soybeans. The first time you do this you will need an adult to show you how to use your can opener, as they are all slightly different. Drain the soybeans in a colander.

2 Using the claw-cutting technique (see page 50), cut the ends off the scallions with a small paring knife and throw away. Cut the scallions into thin slices.

3 Peel the garlic clove and crush it with a garlic press.

4 Put the oil and scallions into a small saucepan over low heat on the stovetop. Heat gently, stirring every now and then with a wooden spoon, until they are soft. This will take about 5 minutes. Add the crushed garlic, ground coriander, and chili powder and cook for another minute.

5 Add the canned tomatoes, drained beans, sugar, and cilantro leaves. Turn the heat up, and when the

tomatoes are bubbling, lower the heat and let simmer gently for 10 minutes.

6 Put the tacos on a baking sheet and, using oven mitts, put them in the oven for 3 minutes to heat up. Scoop the pits out of the avocados with a teaspoon and peel away the skins. Using the claw-cutting technique, cut the avocados into slices. Put the beans, sour cream, cheese, extra cilantro, avocado, and lime in bowls. Let everyone make their own tacos.

rainbow stir-fry

I have used ready-prepared vegetables here so that all you need to prepare are the leeks and green beans, but when you have practiced using a small sharp knife, you may like to add other vegetables like sliced red or yellow peppers or bok choy.

For 4 people you need:

INGREDIENTS
1 leek, trimmed and washed
about 1½ cups green beans
2 large handfuls cilantro leaves
2 garlic cloves
small piece ginger, about 1 inch
2 teaspoons sesame oil
2 teaspoons olive oil
about 10 oz. crunchy vegetable stir-fry mix
(package sizes will vary; the amount doesn't
have to be exact)
10 oz. pre-cooked free-range egg noodles
2 large handfuls pine nuts or peanuts,
if you like
1–2 tablespoons low-salt soy sauce

EQUIPMENT
small paring knife • cutting board
scissors • garlic press • small grater
wok or large frying pan • wooden spoon

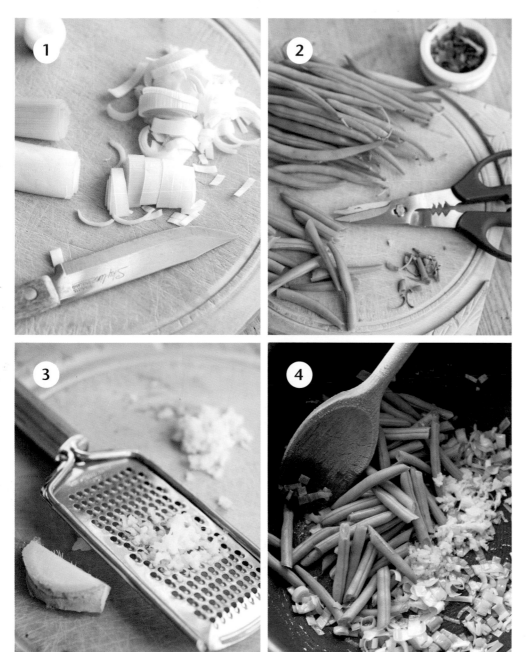

1 Use the bridge-cutting technique to cut the leeks in half widthwise, then lengthwise with a small paring knife. Using the claw-cutting technique, thinly slice the leeks.
2 Using scissors, snip the cilantro into small pieces. Still using scissors, cut the ends off the beans and throw them away. Cut the beans in half.
3 Peel the garlic clove and crush it with a garlic press. Grate the ginger using a small grater (you don't need to peel it first).
4 Turn the burner to medium heat. Heat the oils in a wok or large frying pan. Add the leeks and fry for a few minutes, stirring with a wooden spoon. Add the garlic, ginger, and beans and fry for another minute.
5 Add the vegetable stir-fry mix and fry for another minute. Add the noodles, cilantro, nuts, and soy sauce and fry for a few minutes, stirring as you fry.

5

SKILLS
◆ KNIFE SKILLS
◆ STIR-FRYING
◆ GRATING
◆ CRUSHING
GARLIC
◆ PREPARING
VEGETABLES

how to cook pasta

Knowing how to cook pasta is a great skill, as it is so easy to make it into a lovely meal. However, you will need help from an adult, as the pasta pan will be very heavy and full of hot water!

For 1 person you need:

INGREDIENTS
2½–4 oz. dried pasta

EQUIPMENT
the biggest saucepan you can find ◆ pitcher ◆ long-handled or wooden spoon

a Ideally you need 4 cups of water for every 3½ oz. pasta, but this will only work if you have a pan big enough for this amount of water. However, only ever fill your saucepan three-quarters full. Don't fill it to the top or it will overflow when you add the pasta!

b Find the biggest saucepan that you have in your kitchen (the pasta needs to be cooked in a large pan to help make sure that it cooks evenly; if the pan is too small, some of the pasta may be trapped at the bottom of the pan and it will cook more quickly than the pasta at the top). Turn the burner to medium heat and put the pan of water on it. Heat the water until it comes to a boil—you will know that it is boiling when you can see the water bubbling.

c Put your pasta into a pitcher and then carefully add the pasta to the water (keep your hands away from the hot water!) Using a long-handled spoon, gently swirl the pasta around in the pan to help stop it from sticking together. Bring the water back to a boil and cook following the package instructions (all pastas have different cooking times). Use a fork to take a piece of pasta from the pan, let cool slightly, and then test to see if it is ready: when you bite into it, it should be cooked but still have a little "bite"—this is known as "al dente" in Italy. When it is cooked, put a colander in the sink and ask an adult to pour the pasta into the colander for you (remember, the pan will be very heavy) to drain it.

pasta sauces

pepper pasta sauce

You need to use just plain roasted peppers for this recipe, not antipasti peppers that have lots of oils and herbs added to them.

For 4 people you need:

INGREDIENTS
10 oz. roasted red bell peppers from a jar
10 oz. pasta shapes, cooked and drained (see opposite for instructions)
handful fresh basil or cilantro leaves
handful baby spinach leaves
4 tablespoons cream cheese

EQUIPMENT
colander • scissors • saucepan wooden spoon

Drain the roasted peppers in a colander in the sink. Using scissors, snip the peppers into really small pieces (the smaller the better) and add to the cooked and drained pasta in the saucepan. Tear the basil or cilantro leaves and spinach into small pieces and add to the pasta with the cream cheese. Put the pan over low heat and cook until the cream cheese has melted, stirring gently with a wooden spoon.

tuna pasta sauce

This is one of my daughter Lola's favorite quick suppers, and she also loves it cold in her packed lunchbox for school.

For 4 people you need:

INGREDIENTS
1 cup canned or frozen (and defrosted) corn kernels
2 x 6-oz. cans tuna, drained
3–4 tablespoons mayonnaise
10 oz. pasta shapes, cooked and drained (see opposite for instructions)

EQUIPMENT
can opener • colander • bowl
fork • spoon

Use a can opener to open the can of corn. The first time you do this you will need an adult to show you how to use your can opener, as they all differ slightly. If you are using frozen corn, you will need to let it defrost for at least 1 hour before you make the pasta sauce. Use the can opener to open the cans of tuna. Drain both the corn and tuna in a colander, then tip into a bowl. Break the tuna up with a fork, add the mayonnaise, and mix. Spoon the mixture over the cooked pasta and mix well.

swirly pasta with leek, broccoli, & cheese sauce

It's useful to know how to make a white sauce like this one because it is used in many dishes like lasagne, mac and cheese, cauliflower cheese etc.

1 Turn the oven on to 375°F. Use the claw-cutting technique to cut the broccolini into chunks with a small paring knife. Using the same technique, slice the leek into thin slices.

2 Turn the burner onto low heat. Put the leek and butter into a saucepan on the stovetop and heat gently. Cook for about 10 minutes, or until the leek has softened. Stir with a wooden spoon. Add the flour.

3 Stir and cook for a few minutes until you have a thick paste. Now take a balloon whisk and, whisking all the time, slowly pour in the milk. Keep whisking until you have a smooth sauce and cook gently for a few minutes. Add the mustard and almost all the cheese (keep some for the top) to the sauce, stir, and take off the heat.

4 Cook the pasta following the instructions on page 94. Add the broccolini to the pasta pan 2 minutes before the pasta has finished cooking. When it is cooked, put a colander in the sink and ask an adult to pour the pasta and broccolini into the colander for you. Tip the pasta and broccolini from the colander into an ovenproof dish. Pour the sauce over the top and sprinkle the last bit of cheese over it. Using oven mitts, put the dish in the oven. Cook for 25–30 minutes until the topping is golden and the sauce is bubbling.

For 4 people you need:

INGREDIENTS
10 oz. broccolini
1 leek, trimmed and washed
3 tablespoons unsalted butter
⅓ cup all-purpose flour
2 cups whole milk
1 teaspoon English mustard
2 large handfuls grated cheddar cheese
8 oz. pasta spirals

EQUIPMENT
small paring knife • cutting board
saucepan • wooden spoon • balloon whisk
colander • ovenproof dish • oven mitts

SKILLS
♦ CHOPPING
♦ MAKING WHITE SAUCE
♦ COOKING PASTA
♦ USING OVEN

easy minestrone soup

The great thing about this soup is that you don't have to blend it at the end of cooking. It's ready to eat just as it is, all lovely and chunky.

For 4 people you need:

INGREDIENTS
4 scallions
1 garlic clove
1 tablespoon olive oil
2 cups tomato purée or passata
1 teaspoon sugar
14-oz. can carton soybeans in water
¾ cup small pasta for soup
2 large handfuls frozen peas
2 tablespoons pesto
handful grated Parmesan

EQUIPMENT
*small paring knife ◆ cutting board
rolling pin ◆ garlic press ◆ heavy-based
saucepan ◆ wooden spoon*

1 Using the claw-cutting technique, cut the ends off the scallions with a small paring knife and throw away. Now slice the scallions into thin slices.
2 Bash the garlic clove with a rolling pin, then peel off the skin.
3 Crush the garlic clove using a garlic press.
4 Turn the burner to low heat. Heat the oil in a heavy-based saucepan on the stovetop. Fry the scallions and garlic for 2 minutes, stirring every now and then with a wooden spoon. Pour the tomato purée into the pan. Fill the tomato container with water and pour into the pan. Do this twice. Add the sugar.
5 Add the soybeans. Turn the heat up to high and cook until the mixture is simmering. Lower the heat and simmer gently for 15 minutes.
6 Add the pasta, peas, and pesto and cook for another 5 minutes (or however long the pasta package says). Sprinkle the grated Parmesan on top.

Tip: To add green beans instead of peas, cut the ends off using scissors and compost them (or throw them away), then cut the beans into small pieces before you put them into the soup.

SKILLS
- ◆ CUTTING
- ◆ USING STOVETOP
- ◆ CRUSHING GARLIC
- ◆ USING SCISSORS

STAGE
3

fish curry with rice

Have you ever been to a curry house? You may think that all curries are hot and spicy, but they are not. They can be mild and creamy and taste delicious like this.

For 4 people you need:

INGREDIENTS
big handful cilantro leaves
3 scallions
1 tablespoon olive oil
3 tablespoons mild curry paste
14 oz. canned chopped tomatoes
1 scant cup hot vegetable stock or hot water
large handful few different vegetables e.g. baby corn and green beans
10 oz. mixed fresh fish fillets e.g. haddock, salmon, monkfish, chopped into big chunks, or raw peeled shrimp
cooked long-grain rice (see opposite for instructions)
naan bread, poppadoms, and mango chutney, to serve

EQUIPMENT
scissors • small paring knife • cutting board • large saucepan • wooden spoon

1 Using scissors, snip the cilantro into small pieces. Using the bridge-cutting technique, slice the vegetables in half lengthwise with a small paring knife. Using the claw-cutting technique, cut the ends off the scallions and throw away. Cut the scallions into thin slices. Turn the burner to low heat. Put the scallions and oil in a large saucepan on the stovetop and heat gently.
2 Add the curry paste and fry for a few minutes, stirring with a wooden spoon.
3 Add the canned tomatoes to the pan, then fill the can with the hot stock or water and add to the pan, too. Simmer for 10 minutes, stirring once or twice.
4 Add the vegetables and cook for 5 minutes. Add the fish and cook until the fish is cooked—this will only be 5 minutes, as you don't want to overcook it. Ask an adult to help you check if it is cooked. Add the snipped cilantro and stir. Serve with cooked rice, naan, poppadoms, and chutney.

how to cook rice

For 2 people you need:

INGREDIENTS
1 tall glass of long-grain rice

EQUIPMENT
tall glass ◆ saucepan

a Measure 1 tall glass or cup of rice. Put the rice and then 2 glasses of water into a saucepan. Turn the burner to medium heat and put the pan on the stovetop.

b Bring the water in the pan up to a boil, lower the heat, put the lid on the pan, and simmer for 14 minutes. Ask an adult to help you take the pan off the stovetop and leave for 10 minutes with the lid on. The rice will continue to steam and become fluffy. Don't take the lid off during this time—it is important that the lid stays on if you want fluffy rice.

STAGE
3

super sushi rolls

This looks so impressive and yet it is easy and great fun to make. You will need to look for the ingredients in a good supermarket. Read the cooking instructions on the package of sushi rice before you cook it, but my method below is how most sushi rice is cooked so it's likely to be similar.

1 To cook the rice, put the water and rice into a large saucepan over medium heat on the stovetop. Heat until the water comes to a boil—you will know it is boiling when the water is bubbling. Cover the pan with the lid, lower the heat, and simmer for 10 minutes. Take the pan off the stovetop and let stand for 15 minutes with the lid on. Spoon the rice into a mixing bowl. In a small bowl, mix together the vinegar, sugar, and salt. Pour the vinegar dressing over the rice, mix together, and let cool.

2 Put a sheet of nori seaweed on a sushi mat. Use your hands or a spoon to cover two-thirds of the seaweed with rice. Leave a strip along the end of the seaweed furthest from you without rice. Press the rice down so that it is quite flat and evenly spread out.

3 Put a few strips of avocado and some shrimp along the middle.

4 Pick up the edge of the mat closest to you and roll up the seaweed and its filling into a big sausage. Use the mat to help you roll the seaweed neatly.

5 Squash the roll to make the sushi nice and compact, then unroll the mat. Do all this again with the remaining sheets of seaweed, rice, and filling. Using the claw-cutting technique, cut each roll of sushi into 5 or 6 pieces with a small paring knife and serve with pickled ginger and soy sauce, if you like.

SKILLS
COOKING SUSHI RICE
ROLLING UP SUSHI ◆ CUTTING

5

To make about 30 pieces you need:

RICE
2 cups water
1 generous cup Japanese rice for sushi
2 tablespoons rice wine vinegar
1 tablespoon natural cane sugar
pinch salt
6 sheets nori seaweed

FILLINGS
ripe avocado strips and small, cooked shrimp
OR smoked salmon and thin cucumber strips
OR try thin strips of omelet
You might like to eat your sushi with pickled
ginger and soy sauce

EQUIPMENT ◆ *large saucepan* ◆ *timer*
spoon ◆ *mixing bowl* ◆ *small bowl* ◆ *spoon*
sushi mat ◆ *small paring knife*

STAGE
3

Great granny's smoked haddock & spinach spuds

Have you ever baked a potato before? A good baked potato should have a crisp skin and a light, fluffy middle. To achieve this you will need to bake them for an hour in a hot oven. My granny taught me to make these when I was little. It was the first time I had ever cooked fish and I still remember how good it felt.

For 4 people you need:

INGREDIENTS

4 baking potatoes
3 smoked haddock fillets
a little unsalted butter
2 large handfuls baby spinach leaves
handful fresh herbs e.g. parsley or fennel tops
½ lemon
3 tablespoons sour cream, crème fraîche, or a little butter

EQUIPMENT

fork • ovenproof dish • spoons • oven mitts
timer • scissors • mixing bowl • lemon juicer
fork • table knife • clean napkin • roasting dish

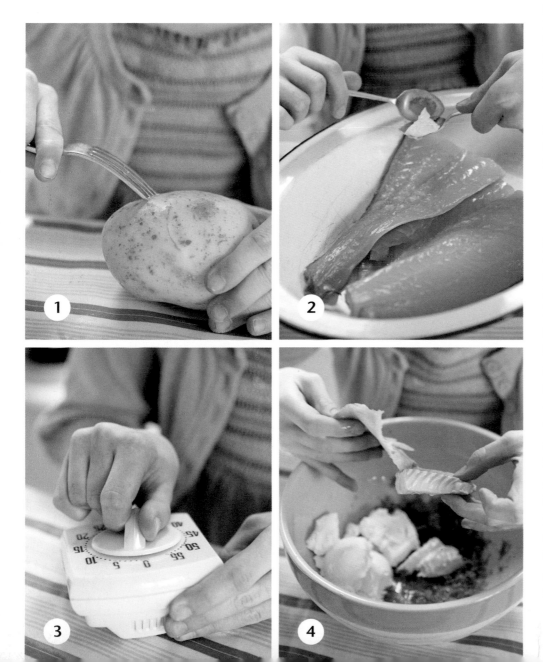

1 Turn the oven on to 375°F. Prick the potatoes all over with a fork.

2 Put the smoked haddock into an ovenproof dish and dot with a little butter using teaspoons.

3 Using oven mitts, put the potatoes as well as the haddock into the oven. Set a timer for 15 minutes. Using oven mitts, take the haddock out of the oven and put to one side. Set the timer for 45 minutes more for the potatoes.

4 Using scissors, snip the herbs into small pieces and put into a mixing bowl. Tear the spinach into small pieces and put to one side. Squeeze the lemon half over a lemon juicer and pour the juice over the herbs. Add the sour cream. When the fish is cool enough to handle, peel the flesh away from the skin and flake the fish into the bowl. Mix everything together with a fork.

5 Using oven mitts, take the potatoes out of the oven. Let cool slightly. Holding a potato with a clean napkin or oven mitt, use a table knife to cut the potato in half. Use a spoon to scoop the middle of the potato out of the potato skin and into the bowl with the haddock and herbs. Squash the chopped spinach into the potato skins. Mix the haddock mixture and cooked potato together in the bowl. Now spoon it back into the potato skins on top of the spinach. You will need to spoon the mixture between the potato skins. Using oven mitts, put the dish back in the oven and set the timer for another 10 minutes. Using oven mitts, take them out of the oven.

SKILLS
- USING SCISSORS
- BAKING POTATOES
- COOKING FISH
- SQUEEZING LEMONS
- USING OVEN
- SHARING

STAGE
3

beef & corn tortilla tubes

These are lots of fun to make and eat! The corn tortillas become all lovely and crisp when you bake them in the oven. (You will need to use corn tortillas, not flour ones). This is delicious with the green dip on page 30.

To make 8 tubes you need:

INGREDIENTS
1 red onion
1 garlic clove
3 carrots, well washed
1 tablespoon olive oil plus a little extra
1 lb. ground beef
2 cups tomato purée or passata
pinch brown sugar
8 corn tortillas
salad and Green Dip (page 30), to serve

EQUIPMENT
small paring knife ◆ cutting board ◆ garlic press grater ◆ frying pan ◆ wooden spoon ◆ ovenproof dish ◆ oven mitts

1 Turn the oven on to 375°F. Peel the onion. Use the bridge-cutting technique to halve it with a paring knife. Using the claw-cutting technique, thinly slice it. Peel the garlic and crush it with a garlic press. Grate the carrots with a grater.
2 Put the oil, onion, garlic, and carrots into a heavy-based frying pan over low heat on the stovetop. Heat until soft.
3 Add the beef and fry for 10 minutes, or until it's turning golden brown. Add the tomato purée and sugar, cover the pan with a lid, and cook gently for 10 minutes. The mixture will be quite dry, which is what you want.
4 Lay the tortillas on the cutting board, then spoon some beef along the middle. Roll the tortillas around the beef and put into an ovenproof dish. Brush the tortilla tubes with a little oil. Using oven mitts, put the dish into the oven and cook for 15 minutes.

SKILLS ◆ CUTTING ◆ CRUSHING GARLIC ◆ FRYING ◆ ROLLING USING OVEN

all-in-one chicken

My girls really enjoy making a meal for the whole family to eat together, but they don't want to always spend long making it. This is why we came up with this recipe idea. To keep it really simple, put some baking potatoes into the oven to cook alongside the chicken. This is delicious with couscous (see page 62), rice (see page 101), or salad (see page 18).

For 4 people you need:
INGREDIENTS
1 cup pitted black olives
10 oz. roasted red peppers from a jar
2 sprigs fresh rosemary
2 tablespoons olive oil
14 oz. canned chopped tomatoes
2 garlic cloves
4 free-range chicken pieces e.g. thighs or legs
baked potatoes, rice, or mashed potatoes, or bread and salad, to serve

EQUIPMENT
colander ◆ scissors
mixing bowl ◆ garlic press
roasting dish ◆ oven mitts

1 Turn the oven on to 350°F. Tip the olives (if they need draining) and roasted peppers into a colander over a mixing bowl to drain. Now pour the liquid out of the bowl.
2 Using scissors, snip the peppers into small pieces and put into the dry mixing bowl.
3 Add the rosemary, olive oil, and canned tomatoes to the peppers, then squash the olives slightly to break them up and add to the bowl, too. Peel the garlic cloves and crush them with a garlic press. Add the crushed garlic to the bowl.

4 Pull the skin off the chicken, throw the skin away, then add the chicken to the bowl.
5 Mix everything with your hands to coat the chicken in the pepper and olive mixture. Now WASH YOUR HANDS. Tip everything into a roasting dish. Using oven mitts, put the dish in the oven and cook for 35–45 minutes (depending on the size of the chicken pieces), or until the chicken is cooked all the way through—ask an adult to help you check this.

SKILLS
* GARLIC CRUSHING
* USING SCISSORS
* USING OVEN

lemony chicken

To make a marinade, you normally mix together an acid, like lemon juice or vinegar with an oil, like olive oil, sunflower oil, or sesame oil. You then add some flavor with chopped herbs, spices, or garlic. The marinade helps to keep the food juicy and stops it from drying out during cooking. This is why people often make a marinade for meat before they barbecue it on a hot grill.

For 4 people you need:

INGREDIENTS

1 garlic clove
1 lemon
6 free-range skinless chicken thigh fillets
2 tablespoons olive oil
2 teaspoons honey
1 teaspoon dried oregano

EQUIPMENT

rolling pin • cutting board small paring knife • lemon juicer • mixing bowl spoon • roasting dish oven mitts

1 Bash the garlic clove with a rolling pin—this will help to loosen the pink papery skin—then peel off the skin. Using the rolling pin again, squash the garlic to crush it slightly—this helps its flavor to come out as it cooks. Remember to wash the rolling pin after!

2 Use the bridge-cutting technique to halve the lemon with a small paring knife. Put a lemon half over a lemon juicer and press down to squeeze out the juice. Repeat with the other lemon half.

3 Put the chicken in a mixing bowl and add the garlic, lemon juice, oil, honey, and dried oregano. Mix with a spoon, cover, and put in the fridge for at least 1 hour. After 1 hour, turn the oven on to 375°F. Spoon the chicken into a roasting dish (leave the marinade behind). Using oven mitts, put the dish in the oven and roast for 25–30 minutes —ask an adult to help you check if it is cooked. Turn the chicken once during this time. Cut the chicken into small pieces to serve.

SKILLS
◆ BASHING GARLIC
◆ CUTTING
◆ MAKING MARINADE
◆ SQUEEZING LEMONS
◆ USING OVEN

STAGE
3

toffee apple tarts

These tarts are so enjoyable to make that the boys who came over to my house to make them for this book asked to make some more in between taking the photos. Once you know how to make pastry dough, you can make so many different pies, cheese straws, small tarts, big tarts, and lots more.

1 Use a table knife to cut the butter into small pieces and put into a mixing bowl with the flour. Rub the butter into the flour with your fingers until it looks like fine bread crumbs. This can take a few minutes.

2 Add the sugar, egg yolk, and water and stir the mixture together with the table knife until it comes together and you can form a ball with your hands. Wrap the pastry in plastic wrap and put it in the fridge for 30 minutes—this will make it easier to roll out.

3 Turn the oven on to 350°F. Using a scrap of parchment paper, rub a little butter inside the holes in the cupcake pans. Break the dough into 4 pieces. Sprinkle a little flour on the work surface, then roll out one piece at a time. Dip the cutter in flour, then cut out 24 circles. Gently press the circles into the holes of the pans.

4 Use the table knife and a cutting board to cut the apples in small pieces, avoiding the core in the middle. Divide the pieces between the dough crusts.

5 Put the toffees on a solid work surface and GENTLY bash with the rolling pin to break into pieces. Scatter the pieces evenly over the apples. Using oven mitts, put the pans in the oven and bake for 15 minutes, or until the toffee has melted and the apples are cooked.

5

To make 24 little tarts you need:

SWEET PIE CRUST DOUGH
1 stick unsalted butter, chilled
1¾ cups all-purpose flour
1 teaspoon sugar
1 egg yolk (see page 84 for separating eggs)
1–2 tablespoons cold water

FILLING
about 6–8 eating apples
12 hard toffee candies

EQUIPMENT
table knife ◆ mixing bowl ◆ plastic wrap
parchment paper ◆ 2 x 12-hole cupcake pans
rolling pin ◆ round cutter about 3 inches across
cutting board ◆ oven mitts

SKILLS
◆ CUTTING
◆ RUBBING BUTTER INTO FLOUR
◆ LINING TART PANS WITH DOUGH
◆ SHARING FILLINGS
◆ BASHING WITH ROLLING PIN
◆ USING OVEN

STAGE
3

scones & jam

Once you know how to make scones, you will always have something for tea or for your packed lunches. Why not treat Mom and Dad and make them a batch at the weekend? Lola's friend Annabelle tested this recipe for me and made them once after breakfast and before school for her and her brother's packed lunches! Well done Annabelle!

To make 8–10 scones you need:

INGREDIENTS
1¾ cups self-rising flour
1 teaspoon baking powder
2½ tablespoons unsalted butter, chilled
1 tablespoon sugar
⅔ cup milk plus a little extra
strawberry jam, to serve

EQUIPMENT
scissors • parchment paper baking sheet • mixing bowl table knife • round fluted cutter about 2¼ inches across pastry brush • oven mitts

1 Turn the oven on to 425°F. Cut a piece of parchment paper big enough to cover the baking sheet. Put the flour and baking powder into a mixing bowl. Use a table knife to cut the butter into small pieces and put into the mixing bowl with the flour. Rub the butter into the flour with your fingers until it looks like fine bread crumbs. This can take a few minutes, so be patient and keep going!

2 Add the sugar and milk. Use a table knife to stir and start to mix everything together.

3 Now use your hands to bring the mixture together to make a ball of dough.

4 Sprinkle a little flour on the work surface, then tip the dough out of the bowl. Pat it gently to flatten until it is about ⅔ inch thick. Dip the cutter in flour, then cut out scones from the dough. Put the scones onto the baking sheet, spaced a little apart. Gather all the spare bits of dough together, roll together to make a ball, and flatten out again. Cut out the rest of the scones—you should be able to make 8, 9, or 10 scones depending on the size of your cutter.

5 Dip a pastry brush into a little milk and brush over the scones. Using oven mitts, put the scones in the oven and bake for 10 minutes until risen and golden.

Let cool slightly before cutting in half and serving with strawberry jam and cream, if you like it.

Other good things to add to scones: For fruit scones add ½ cup dried fruit, such as raisins or currants or chopped dried apricots or apple. Stir in when you add the sugar. Try adding a pinch of apple pie spice or cinnamon. For cheesy scones, leave out the sugar and stir in ½ cup grated hard cheese and chopped fresh herbs.

SKILLS
◆ RUBBING BUTTER INTO FLOUR
◆ CUTTING USING CUTTERS
◆ BRUSHING (MILK) USING PASTRY BRUSH

STAGE
3

roasted fruit

When you bake fruit in the oven, the key is to not overcook it otherwise it will get too soft. The times will vary depending on the size of the fruit, but 15 minutes is good for large soft fruits like nectarines or peaches. If you choose smaller fruit like plums, cook them for just 10 minutes. Roasted fruits are great served with plain yogurt. For a treat, add half a teaspoon of heavy cream to each fruit half before baking so that you have a sauce at the end of the cooking time.

For 4 people you need:

INGREDIENTS
4 peaches or nectarines, or 8 plums or apricots
3 tablespoons light brown sugar
capful almond or vanilla extract
2 tablespoons unsalted butter

EQUIPMENT
cutting board ◆ small paring knife ◆ spoon
ovenproof dish ◆ oven mitts

1 Turn the oven on to 375°F. Use the bridge-cutting technique to cut the fruit in half: on a cutting board, make a "bridge" with a thumb and finger of one hand and hold the fruit. Hold a small paring knife in your other hand and put the blade under the bridge, then cut downwards firmly. You will need to move the fruit around as you cut to avoid cutting through the pit. This will take a bit of time, patience, and practice.

2 Use a teaspoon to scoop the pits out of the middle of the fruit. You might need to dig the spoon under the pit to take it out.

3 Rest the fruit in an ovenproof dish with the cut side facing up. Spoon the sugar evenly over each fruit half, add the almond extract, and dot with little pieces of the butter. Using oven mitts, put the dish in the oven and bake for 15–20 minutes. I think these peaches look so beautiful, don't you?

SKILLS
- ◆ CUTTING
- ◆ PITTING FRUIT
- ◆ USING OVEN

STAGE
3

magic citrus desserts

These desserts are light and fluffy on top, with a pool of lemon sauce at the bottom. They are delicate because of the egg white, and that's why they need to be cooked in a roasting dish with water around them to help them cook slowly.

For 4–5 people you need:
INGREDIENTS
1 unwaxed lemon and 1 unwaxed lime
(or just 2 lemons or limes, if you like)
½ cup natural cane sugar
3½ tablespoons unsalted butter, soft
2 free-range eggs
½ cup plus 1 tablespoon self-rising flour
1 cup milk
EQUIPMENT
small grater • mixing bowl • wooden spoon • saucer • 2 bowls • balloon whisk small paring knife • electric mixer • metal spoon • 4–5 small pudding basins • deep roasting pan • small pitcher • oven mitts

1 Turn the oven on to 350°F. Using a small grater, grate the lemon and lime to make zest (see page 60 for how to do this) and put into a mixing bowl. Add the sugar and butter and mix well with a wooden spoon until it becomes fluffy and paler in color. Crack an egg onto a saucer (see page 60 for how to do this), rest a small bowl over the yolk and tip the white into a clean bowl*. Add the egg yolk to the butter mixture in the mixing bowl and then repeat with the other egg.

2 Add the flour to the mixing bowl and, using a balloon whisk, mix together. Use the bridge-cutting technique to halve the zested lemon with a small paring knife. Squeeze the juice into the mixing bowl, add the milk, and whisk.

3 Using a clean balloon whisk or an electric mixer (with help from an adult), whisk the eggs whites in their bowl until they are thick, white, and make slight peaks.

SKILLS
◆ GRATING
◆ SEPARATING EGGS
◆ FOLDING
◆ WHISKING EGG WHITES

4 Using a metal spoon, "fold" the egg whites into the batter in the mixing bowl. "Folding" means to carefully cut the batter and mix without beating all the air out of the egg whites. Fold until the whites are just mixed in.

5 Rub a little butter inside 4–5 small pudding basins and put them in a deep roasting pan. Spoon the batter into the basins, then pour water from a small pitcher into the roasting pan to come halfway up the sides of the basins. Ask an adult to help you put the pan in the oven using oven mitts. Bake for 35 minutes, or until the desserts are golden and cooked with a small pool of sauce in the bottom. *Did you know that the bowl for egg whites needs to be really clean, otherwise you might not end up with fluffy egg whites?

STAGE
3

blackberry pudding

This is as easy as 1, 2, 3. Measure the ingredients, mix them together, and then bake. I have chosen to use ground almonds and light cream in this recipe for a really special dessert. However, if you don't have ground almonds you could use self-rising flour and instead of cream you can use milk. It will not have the same flavor or texture, but it's still a nice dessert. You could also try to make this dessert with other fruits that are in season e.g. soft fruits like raspberries, sliced fresh peaches, plum halves or apricot halves, or mixed fruit like raspberries mixed with red currants and black currants.

For 4 people you need:

INGREDIENTS
2½ tablespoons unsalted butter
3 free-range eggs
a scant ½ cup natural cane sugar
capful vanilla extract
⅔ cup light cream
1 cup ground almonds
2 baskets blackberries
a little sugar for the top

EQUIPMENT
parchment paper • medium ovenproof dish • small saucepan • table knife pitcher • fork • oven mitt

1 Turn the oven on to 350°F. Using a scrap of parchment paper, rub a little butter inside the ovenproof dish. Put the butter in a small saucepan over low heat on the stovetop and heat gently until it has melted. Crack the eggs into a pitcher (see page 60 for how to do this) and measure all the other ingredients.

2 Add the melted butter, sugar, vanilla extract, cream, and ground almonds to the eggs in the pitcher and mix together with a fork. Pour this batter into your ovenproof dish.

3 Dot the blackberries all over the batter. Using oven mitts, put the dish into the oven and bake for 30–35 minutes or until the pudding is cooked all the way through. It tastes great with ice cream or yogurt or on its own!

SKILLS
- ◆ MELTING BUTTER
- ◆ MIXING
- ◆ MEASURING
- ◆ USING OVEN

STAGE
3

Ella's raspberry & white chocolate cake

Ella is the queen of sponge cakes in our house and this light yellow cake is based on the classic Victoria sponge cake—named after the queen herself! It was Ella's idea to add fresh raspberries to the batter and to make some lovely big white chocolate buttons for the top. I hope you enjoy making it as much she did!

To make 1 big cake you need:

CAKE BASE

3½ oz. white chocolate
almost 2 sticks unsalted butter, soft
1 generous cup natural cane sugar
capful vanilla extract
4 eggs, at room temperature
1¾ cups self-rising flour
14 oz. ripe raspberries (or fruits of the forest) plus extra to decorate
1 teaspoon baking powder
4 tablespoons raspberry jam

BUTTERCREAM

6½ tablespoons unsalted butter, soft
1 cup confectioners' sugar
3 ripe raspberries

ICING

3 ripe raspberries
2 cups confectioners' sugar
a little water

EQUIPMENT

2 plates • parchment paper • small saucepan • small heatproof bowl • oven mitts • spoon • 2 x 8-inch cake pans pencil • scissors • 3 mixing bowls wooden spoon • table knife • large metal spoon • fork

1 Cover a big plate with parchment paper. Half fill a small saucepan with water and sit a small heatroof bowl in the pan over the water (without the bowl touching the water). Break the chocolate into the small bowl. Put the pan over low heat on the stovetop. When the water starts to heat up, the chocolate will melt. Don't touch the chocolate—leave it until it has melted. Turn the burner off and carefully, using oven mitts, take the bowl off the pan and stir the chocolate. Spoon circles of the chocolate onto the parchment paper and leave somewhere cold to set.

5

6

7

2 Turn the oven on to 350°F. Using a scrap of parchment paper, rub a little butter inside the cake pans. Rest one pan on some parchment paper and draw around the pan with a pencil. Cut 2 circles out and put in the bottom of the pans.

3 Put the soft butter, sugar, and vanilla extract in a mixing bowl and mix well with a wooden spoon until it becomes fluffy and paler in color. Crack the eggs and add to the batter a little a time, mixing all the time. Add just a little flour, too.

4 Add the raspberries and gently mix together. Don't worry if the batter looks slightly lumpy or curdled—this is normal.

5 Add the flour and, using a large metal spoon, "fold" it into the batter. "Folding" means to carefully cut the batter and mix without beating all the air out of it.

6 Spoon the batter equally into the pans. Using oven mitts, put the pans in the oven and bake for 20 minutes, or until the cakes are well risen and cooked through.

7 Using the oven mitts, take the cakes out of the oven. Let cool, then turn them out of the pans and peel the paper off. To make the buttercream, put the butter, sugar, and raspberries in a bowl and mix until really smooth. Put one of the cakes onto a plate and spread the jam over it. Spread the buttercream over the jam and put the other cake on top. To make the icing, mash the raspberries in a bowl with a fork, add the confectioners' sugar and a little water, and mix together. Spoon onto the cake and decorate with more raspberries and the white chocolate buttons.

SKILLS
**MEASURING ♦ CREAMING
BUTTER & SUGAR ♦ CRACKING
EGGS ♦ FOLDING FLOUR
SPREADING ♦ MELTING
CHOCOLATE**

STAGE
3

pick 'n' mix hot choc

For a really special hot chocolate, you can just melt chocolate into milk like Ella is doing here and then add flavor from orange zest or a spice. Otherwise, you can use sweetened cocoa mix. This is a great recipe for making when you have friends over. You can create your own "drinks bar" with little bowls of spices or orange zest for flavor, and candies and chocolates for the top. Your friends are likely to have great fun choosing what to add to their hot chocolates. Enjoy!

To make 1 hot chocolate you need:

HOT CHOCOLATE
milk

a few squares milk chocolate or 2 teaspoons sweetened cocoa mix

FLAVOURING
freshly grated ginger, ground cinnamon, grated orange zest

TOPPING
whipped cream in a can (or whipped heavy cream)

a selection of candies e.g. white chocolate buttons, milk chocolate buttons, mini-marshmallows, chocolate flakes, sprinkles

EQUIPMENT
cup • small saucepan wooden spoon • spoon

1 Measure the milk in the cup you will be using—pour the milk into your cup and then pour this milk into a small saucepan. Only three-quarters fill your cup, as you will need room for the toppings!
2 Add the chocolate to the pan and heat until it melts and the milk just starts to bubble—don't leave it too long otherwise the milk will rise up inside the pan and spill over the top! Take the pan off the heat. Stir with a wooden spoon until the chocolate has melted.

3 Pour the hot chocolate into your cup.
4 Now decide which flavor you would like to add to your hot chocolate—freshly grated ginger, ground cinnamon, and grated orange zest are all good—and stir it in. Top the hot chocolate with whipped cream and chocolates and sprinkles. My children like to add a flake too!

SKILLS
MEASURING • POURING • GRATING

124

index

conversion chart

Weights and measures have been rounded up or down slightly to make measuring easier.

Measuring butter:
A US stick of butter weighs 4 oz. which is approximately 115 g or 8 tablespoons.

American	Metric	Imperial
6 tbsp	85 g	3 oz.
7 tbsp	100 g	3½ oz.
1 stick	115 g	4 oz.

The recipes in this book require the following conversions:

Volume equivalents:

American	Metric	Imperial
1 teaspoon	5 ml	
1 tablespoon	15 ml	
¼ cup	60 ml	2 fl. oz.
⅓ cup	75 ml	2½ fl. oz.
½ cup	125 ml	4 fl. oz.
⅔ cup	150 ml	5 fl. oz. (¼ pint)
¾ cup	175 ml	6 fl. oz.
1 cup	250 ml	8 fl. oz.

Weight equivalents:

Imperial	Metric
1 oz.	30 g
2 oz.	55 g
3 oz.	85 g
3½ oz.	100 g
4 oz.	115 g
6 oz.	175 g
8 oz. (½ lb.)	225 g
9 oz.	250 g
10 oz.	280 g
12 oz.	350 g
13 oz.	375 g
14 oz.	400 g
15 oz.	425 g
16 oz. (1 lb.)	450 g

Measurements:

Inches	cm
¼ inch	5 mm
½ inch	1 cm
1 inch	2.5 cm
2 inches	5 cm
3 inches	7 cm
4 inches	10 cm
5 inches	12 cm
6 inches	15 cm
7 inches	18 cm
8 inches	20 cm
9 inches	23 cm
10 inches	25 cm
11 inches	28 cm
12 inches	30 cm

Oven temperatures:

120°C	(250°F)	Gas ½
140°C	(275°F)	Gas 1
150°C	(300°F)	Gas 2
170°C	(325°F)	Gas 3
180°C	(350°F)	Gas 4
190°C	(375°F)	Gas 5
200°C	(400°F)	Gas 6
220°C	(425°F)	Gas 7

SKIRA

TEXT AND COLOR PLATES PRINTED BY
IRL IMPRIMERIES RÉUNIES LAUSANNE S.A.

BINDING BY
MAYER & SOUTTER S.A. RENENS

PRINTED IN SWITZERLAND